PRAISE FOR
THE BEDWETTER

"The strange combination of irreverent silliness and un-diluted earnestness makes *The Bedwetter* more than just funny business."   —*Entertainment Weekly*

"It's irreverent, funny, and sometimes winningly serious."
                                    —*Los Angeles Times*

"Often hilarious and occasionally revelatory."
                                    —*New York Times*

"Deftly mixes the spit-take funny stuff with an unsentimental but enlightened look back at her not-so-charmed life and career."   —*Vanity Fair*

"The risqué comedienne's memoir does not disappoint in the laughs department. But there are also some surprisingly poignant moments that give this book real heart."
                                    —*Cosmopolitan*

THE
BEDWETTER

STORIES OF COURAGE, REDEMPTION, AND PEE

SARAH SILVERMAN

itbooks

AN IMPRINT OF HARPERCOLLINS PUBLISHERS

*it***books**

A few names have been changed so
I don't hurt anyone's feelings or get sued.

A hardcover edition of this book was published in 2010 by HarperCollins Publishers.

THE BEDWETTER. Copyright © 2010 by Sarah Silverman. All rights reserved. Printed in the United States of America. No part of this book may be used or reproduced in any manner whatsoever without written permission except in the case of brief quotations embodied in critical articles and reviews. For information, address HarperCollins Publishers, 10 East 53rd Street, New York, NY 10022.

HarperCollins books may be purchased for educational, business, or sales promotional use. For information, please write: Special Markets Department, HarperCollins Publishers, 10 East 53rd Street, New York, NY 10022.

First It Books edition published 2011.

Library of Congress Cataloging-in-Publication Data has been applied for.

ISBN 978-0-06-185645-7

11 12 13 14 15   OV/RRD   10 9 8 7 6 5 4 3 2

For my family. I am so proud to be a part of us.

In loving memory of John O'Hara.

CONTENTS

THE
BEDWETTER

FOREWORD

by Sarah Silverman

When I first selected myself to write the foreword for my book, I was flattered, and deeply moved. It is not every day that someone is asked to write the foreword for such a highly anticipated book by a major publisher. There was a time in my life that I would not have trusted myself with a responsibility like this. The foreword sets the tone for the entire book, and I might well have said, "Sarah, you're not smart enough to handle this." I would have taken the safer route, and just asked someone other than myself to write it. To trust myself this much, to think so highly of my own literary skills, is a testament to just how far I've come—both personally and professionally. Personally, because I'm finally in a place where I can really look up to myself, and professionally, because I'm now able to see what a coup getting me to write my foreword really is.

Not everyone agrees that I should be writing this thing. Take, for example, the people at HarperCollins. They're staunchly opposed to it. Old media traditionalists that they are, they seem to be stuck on the idea that a foreword should be written by someone *other* than the author. They even went so far as to claim that the very *point* of a foreword is to have someone else writing about the author. Here's an excerpt of an e-mail chain between my editor and me regarding the issue.

From: David Hirshey

To: Sarah Silverman
Date: July 2, 2009
Re: Foreword

Hi Sarah—
Can we talk about the foreword? I really don't think it makes any sense for you to write it yourself.

Stay Jewish,
David

On July 3, 2009, Sarah Silverman wrote:

You are dumb and smell fartish.

Best wishes,
Sarah

From: David Hirshey

To: Sarah
Date: July 3, 2009
Subject: Re: Foreword

Dear Sarah:
I'm sorry that our last discussion regarding the foreword issue was upsetting to you. If you perceived a lack of sympathy, or any recalcitrance

on our part, it is because your suggestion took us a bit by surprise. No one in our history—and we researched this—has ever proposed that they write the foreword to their own memoir. It's a complete contradiction in logic.

Best,
David

In other words, I guess he's saying that if it was me writing, it would not really be a true "foreword," it would simply be the start of the book, thus making the book effectively foreword-less. I would argue that, if this book is foreword-less, how can you be reading this at this very moment? That said, if you aren't reading this, I can't blame you, since I've said literally nothing so far.

✳   ✳   ✳

Now, then.

I have known Sarah (me) for thirty-nine years. I have watched her grow from a flat-chested, gawky little blastocyst into a full-grown woman with big naturals and a major career. Her contributions have ranged from telling offensive racial jokes in dingy comedy clubs to playing a decisive role in getting the first person of color elected president. She has peed on mattresses up and down the Northeast Corridor and has used the topic of human excrement to vault her from obscurity into the global fame she enjoys today. Her life has been an inspiration, and I look *foreword* (!!!) to seeing what she does next. With her tremendous reserves of talent, Sarah just might cure AIDS, or at least cause it in deserving people like those genocidal dinks in Darfur. She might become the first Jewish president, or win the NASCAR award if something like that exists, or start some kind of movement. Or *stop* some movement that's especially annoying. Like those people who denounce circumcision and insist on ruining penises across the globe. I guess the effort to *stop* a movement could be called a "Removement." That's a horrible joke. The first thing Sarah should do with her powers is to put a stop to jokes like that. Sarah is the embodiment of possibility and promise. I love her.

Wow. Now, that's a foreword. Egg on your face much, Harper-Collins?

Okay, I just read this over and I have to be honest—I'm maybe coming off a touch insecure. A hair overcompensate-y. Maybe it's because I don't want to accept the hard truth about my precious book, which is that you are most likely going to be reading this, my freshman literary effort, while making a bowel movement. There's one birthing its way out of you at this very moment, isn't there? It's okay. In fact, I'm happy for you, and I'm honored that you've chosen to bring me into this very private and vulnerable part of your life. For all you know, I'm making one as I write this, except that I can tell you with all certainty that I don't do that. Ever. My asshole is as clean as a whistle. (Whistles are traditionally filled with gym-teacher saliva and women-who-fear-they-might-get-raped spit. So, yeah, that's the level of clean. You can see this is not a bragging thing . . .)

I'm not a literary genius. I'm not Dostoyevsky, whoever that is—I'm pretty sure I just made that name up. I'm only thirty-nine years old, with most of my final two years of show business still ahead of me. I was not an orphan. I have never blown anyone for coke or let other people do coke off any part of my body. I have never struggled with addiction and I was never molested. Tragically, my life has only been moderately fucked up. I'm not writing this book to share wisdom or to inspire people. I'm writing this book because I am a famous comedian, which is how it works now. If you're famous, you get to write a book, and not the other way around, so the next Dave Eggers better get a TV show or kill someone or something.

But I will say that my life has been interesting and often outright hilarious, so if you take it just one poop at a time, I think you'll find the journey worthwhile.

I will give you the same advice about your poop that I give myself while writing this very book: Don't push.

Now wipe thoroughly, wash your hands—boil them if you have to—and I'll see you back here tomorrow morning after your cigarette and coffee.

Love,
Sarah

CURSED FROM
THE START

My Life Started by Exploding Out of My Father's
Balls, and You Wonder Why I Work Blue

Like most children, I learned to swear from a parent. But most children learn to swear by mimicking moments when a parent loses self-control. That is typically followed by the parent stressing that such words are bad and shouldn't be repeated outside the home. When I was three years old, I learned to swear from my father, but he taught me with every intention to do so. It was like he was teaching a "cursing as a second language" course for one.

"Bitch! Bastard! Damn! Shit!" I proclaimed with joy, if not necessarily wit, in the middle of Boys' Market in Manchester, New Hampshire. Random shoppers stopped in the aisle, and watched me with delight—or at least curiosity—as I regurgitated this mantra. Dad stood by with genuine pride, beaming through the mock surprise on his face.

Dad and me circa 1975. I believe we were laughing at a comment I made about how his nipple is reminiscent of Van Gogh's Starry Night.

My guess is that when something is so easy, so greatly rewarded, and bears so few negative consequences, it's a recipe for addiction. From that moment on, everything I did was in search of that rush. So I guess I'm saying that I'm, in most ways, my father's fault. He filled my mother's vagina with the filthy semen that consisted of me, then filled my head with even more filth.

✳   ✳   ✳

When I was four I sat coloring a piece of typing paper during a dinner party at my Nana and Papa's house in Concord. It was a white ranch house perched on a hill with long concrete steps leading up to the front door. The living room had bright turquoise carpeting under a long white couch. A blue-and-white candy-filled bowl rested on a thick-glass coffee table. Nana, a fashionable woman in her late fifties, who rocked hot pink lipstick under a swirly mane of salt-and-pepper cotton candy, came out of the kitchen carrying a tray of her famous brownies.

"Sarah, Nana made brownies for you!" she beamed in the third person.

I looked up from my drawing, glanced over to my father, who gave me the nod, then turned to Nana.

"Shove 'em up your ass," I said.

The tide of the guests' laughter quickly swept away any anger Nana had toward Dad. She had to smile. Remembering this very early time makes me nostalgic for the days when naked obscenity was enough for a laugh, and didn't need any kind of crafted punch line to accompany it. It was good to be four.

It strikes me that, in this story of a little girl telling her loving grandmother to shove baked goods up her ass, I might come across as a monster. But allow me to place this anecdote in a cultural context: It was the 1970s. Countless friends of mine who grew up in that decade tell stories of their parents giving them liquor, or pot, or buying them *Playboy* magazines, or letting their boyfriends sleep over at very young ages. Or having "key parties" and orgies while they believed their children were upstairs sleeping. Like oversexualized retarded adults, the 1970s had the distinction of being both naive and inappropriate. For a naive and inappropriate girl to be born from it, it's really not so crazy.

What I said to my grandmother yielded a strange kind of glory, and I basked in it. The reactions were verbally disapproving, but there was an unmistakable encouragement under it all. No meant yes.

He Farts in the Face of Strangers

My father, Donald Silverman, is a black-haired, dark-skinned Jew who walks exactly like Bill Cosby dances. A little bounce with each step, elbows bent with hands dangling at the wrists on either side of his chest. When you see him approach, you might think, "A ridiculous man is walking toward me." And you'd be right.

My dad is pretty much fearless, which makes him a natural showman and public speaker. He's always the one asked to make a toast or a speech. But a perceived fearlessness can sometimes be mistaken for what is actually gall. This is clearly exemplified by my father's willingness to steal all his material. He would lift bits from comedians, songs, sitcoms—anywhere—then tweak them to fit and claim them as his own. He once spoke at the Bar Mitzvah of his friend's son David.

"Today, David, I find in being Jewish a thing of beauty, a joy, a strength, a cup of gladness, a Jewish kingdom as wonderful as any other. Accept in full the sweetness of your Jewishness. David, be brave. Keep freedom in the family and do what you can to make the world a better place. Now may the Constitution of the United States go with you, the Declaration of Independence stand by you, the Bill of Rights protect you. And may your own dreams be your only boundaries henceforth now and forever. Amen."

Tears. Not a dry eye in the house. People flocked to Dad to tell him how moving and brilliant his words were. Evidently, they had never seen the play *Purlie Victorious* by Ossie Davis, because that's where those words were first heard. On Broadway. Other than changing all the instances of "black" to "Jew," my father stole the passage pretty much word for word.

✻   ✻   ✻

My dad was born in Boston, Massachusetts, before moving to New Hampshire where his family settled. His Boston accent is as thick as a stack of ten lobsters and he is almost entirely impossible to understand. My sisters and I became adept at translating what he said into English. *Caaah* was "car," *shaht* was "short," etc. This was a good system, though one that occasionally backfired, causing us to say "parker" or "sofer" in places where he actually was pronouncing something accurately, like, *"Get your parka off the sofa."* My father says *fuckin'* the way people say, "like" or "totally." He might say it in anger like the rest of the world, but what makes him special is he evokes it in everyday talk. "I had such a fuckin' great time." "I'm such a fuckin' lucky daddy." Or, referring to his favorite HBO series, "Is that Ahliss [*Arli$$*, the HBO classic] fuckin' wild o'ah what?"

Happily, Dad found a career that perfectly suited his personality. He owned a store called Crazy Sophie's Factory Outlet. Much like a certain "Eddie" of legend, who perceived the unlikely connection between psychiatric disorder and retail sales volume, Dad did his own radio ads as "Crazy Donald." They were highly spirited—and like everything else that came from his mouth, unintelligible— pitches which went something like,

> *"When I see the prices at the mawl I just want to vawmit. Hi. I'm Crazy Donald, Crazy Sophie's husband."*

Dad would list all the brands of jeans he had in his store— brands I've never since heard of, like Unicorn. At the end he would say either,

"So, spend you-ah time at the mawl, spend you-ah money at Crazy Sophie's!"

or:

"So if you cay-ah enough to buy the very best—but yo-uah too CHEAP, come to Crazy Sophie's!"

In fact, Dad was not Crazy Sophie's husband. Sophie did not exist. He invented her. He wanted a woman's name because he was selling women's clothes. Dad's mother, my Nana, Rose, yelled at him after he named the store, insisting, "You named the store after my friend Sophie Moskowitz, and she will be very insulted!" Dad insisted, "I did not name the sto-ah aftah Sophie Moskowitz. If I named the sto-ah aftah Sophie Moskowitz, I would have named it Ugly Sophie's." Classic.

*   *   *

When my father first came home from college, he sat my grandparents down to tell them some very serious news. They followed him quizzically into the living room, and from the bantam couch stared up at their nervous, pacing son.

"I'm gay," he announced.

They sat stunned for a moment, and just as his mother started to cry he said,

"Just kidding. I smoke."

Genius.

*   *   *

The neighbor's dog was repeatedly shitting in our yard. For a common problem like that, there's a sensible solution: to drop by the neighbor's house and ask, "Would you mind curbing your dog?"

But Dad didn't say a word to the neighbors. Instead, he got up in the middle of the night, gingerly maneuvered the feces onto a piece of cardboard—careful not to disturb its signature shape—tiptoed to the neighbor's driveway, and transferred it onto the pavement just below the driver's-side door of our neighbor's car. It was worth it to him to be nearer to this canine excrement than one would ever need to be, in exchange for the *possibility* that our neighbor would step in his own dog's shit on his way to work.

✻   ✻   ✻

My parents were enjoying hot fudge sundaes at an ice cream parlor called Rumpelmayer's in New York City. A man at the adjacent table was smoking. Since my mother was eight months pregnant (with my eldest sister, Susie), my father asked him if he'd put out his cigarette.

"Fuck off," the man suggested.

My father kept his eyes trained on the man as he instructed my mother to go wait by the front door. He then sidled up to him as close as he could, lifted his leg, and twisted as he sang, "Puff on *this*," which was followed by the most putrid blast of human gas known to man at that time, and was not exceeded until the late '80s by the great violinist Yo-Yo Ma.

The Reason I Am Not Completely Retarded

My mother, Beth Ann, is fair-skinned with green-blue eyes, soft brown hair, and a God-given nose most Jews would pay thousands for. She speaks beautifully and with great passion for proper grammar and pronunciation. Books—real books by fancy book writers—are read with pen in hand to correct typos and grammar mishaps—and she finds them. She's a real-life Diane Chambers. She didn't care if we said "fuck" or "shit" as long as it was with crisp diction and perfect pronunciation.

My mother, Beth Ann, in 1977

When we were kids she marched up to the counter of our local movie theater to complain that the voice on the recording (this is way before Moviefone) was so garbled she couldn't make out what movies were playing. The guy just shrugged and said, *"You* wanna do it?" A star was born.

Mom would take me to the tiny room where the popcorn was stored. There were gigantic bags of pre-popped, yellowed, and packaged popcorn, taken out in increments and placed in the popcorn machine out front to simulate freshness (and also be heated by a lightbulb). The popcorn room was where she would tape the recording of the week's movies, and here, she quietly put her values into practice. Giving such care to each word, her beautiful voice was clear and articulate with just a hint of whisper—like a Connecticut-born Julie Andrews. She expected from herself what she would expect from anyone: perfection. And she did those recordings over and over until she achieved it.

"Thank you for calling Bedford Mall Cinemas 1, 2, 3, and 4, where all bargain matinees are only two dollars Monday through Saturday. Now playing, *Ordinary People*, directed by Robert Redford! . . ."

Instead of a cash payment, we were all allowed to go to the movies for free, plus one, anytime we wanted.

In May of 1964, my mother-to-be (at this point she's borne only my eldest sister, Susie) got on the game show *Concentration*, with Hugh Downs. She won the first two games, then came back the next day and won two more. When she repeated her success on day three she automatically became a contestant in that fall's "Challenge of Champions."

She remembers winning some SCUBA gear and that Hugh Downs asked her smugly if she knew that SCUBA was an acronym and what the letters stood for. She immediately answered, "Self-Contained Underwater Breathing Apparatus?" To which, according to my mother, he blanched and said a very small, "Yes." She said she didn't even know she knew that information until it came out of her mouth. She was twenty-three.

Among the stuff she won was:

a Triumph Spitfire sports car

a dozen leather handbags (all of them yellow)

a twenty-foot speedboat

a twenty-seven-foot "party barge"

two outboard motors for the boats

a mink stole

100 pounds of coffee

a dozen pairs of men's pants

20 pairs of men's shoes

a suite of living room furniture (some of which, forty-five years later, can
   still be found in the house I grew up in—a bachelor's chest on my step-
   father's side of the bed, two maple end tables, and a large hassock in the
   living room)

and

a cruise to Bermuda

Other than those pieces of furniture and the fancy cruise, my parents sold the prizes for cash and with it bought their first house, in Manchester, New Hampshire. Since my mother was pregnant with kid number two, they decided to wait until a few months after the baby was born to take the cruise.

The First Time I Bombed

My parents' second child, Jeffrey Michael Silverman, was born on February 9, 1965.

That May, Donald and Beth Ann went to New York City to

take their cruise to Bermuda, after which they returned to New York to spend the weekend at the World's Fair in Flushing, with their friends Ellie and Harry Bluestein before heading home to New Hampshire. Susie, who had just turned two, was staying with my mother's parents in Connecticut, and the baby, Jeffrey, was in Concord with my father's parents (Nana and Papa), Rose and Max. When they arrived at their hotel near the fairgrounds in Flushing, my father called his parents to check on Jeffrey.

My mother heard my father say, "Gone? What do you mean, 'gone'? Where is he?"

She walked over to him, "What's going on?"

He listened a few moments longer, then collapsed into tears, which curled into wails of despair. Jeffrey was dead.

Donald and Beth Ann arrived at the Concord house, where many friends had gathered around weeping, inconsolable Rose and Max. When Max looked up and saw my parents, he cried out, "How can you forgive me?"

My parents were told that Jeffrey had been crying a lot during the night and that Papa was the one to keep checking on him, since Nana was hard of hearing and couldn't hear him cry. In the morning Papa got up and went to look in on the baby. He got to the crib and didn't see him. He called to Nana, saying, "Rose, where's the baby?" Then they both found him, down in one corner of the port-a-crib. The metal support frame had slipped off its peg, allowing a little narrow space between the mattress and the bottom rail of the crib. My parents were told that he had strangled in that space.

Any concept of closure, if it existed in the '60s at all, was a notion invented by hippie fruits. My parents' friends cleaned up any sign of Jeffrey's existence by the time they got home. He was imagined.

✻   ✻   ✻

In 1976 I was five and cute as a really hairy button. My eldest sister, Susie, was twelve. She was fair with very long dark brown hair and big brown sad eyes reflecting a heartbreaking need for love—by any means necessary.

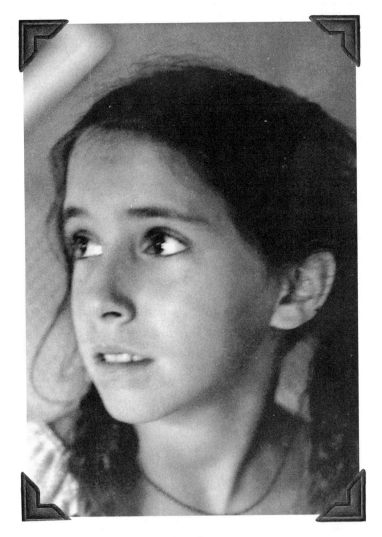

Sweet Susie

When I was three she would babysit me and say, "If I drink this orange juice I'm gonna turn into a monster!"

I'd cry, "Susie no!" But she drank the juice anyway, went into the closet where the washer-dryer was, put a brown suede ski mask on her head, and came back out, monstrafied.

"*RAAAAARGH!!* The only way I'll turn back to Susie is if you hug me!!!"

Terrified, I ran in a burst toward the monster, hugging her, eyes clenched.

Susie once pulled a steak knife out of the silverware drawer, turned to me, and mused, "It's so weird, like, I could kill you right now. Like, I *wouldn't*, but I could. I could just take your life . . ." One way to interpret this is that it foretold her eventual future as a rabbi. At age fourteen, here she was, already pondering the biggest issues of the human condition—life, death, morality, and the choices we must make. An alternate interpretation is that living with me eventually causes one to contemplate murder. But I'm feeling the former explanation is the right one, as it is a scientific certainty that I'm pretty adorable.

✳   ✳   ✳

Laura, a.k.a. "Mowgli"

Laura was in the middle. She was eleven. A tomboy, she looked just like Mowgli from *The Jungle Book*.

She had olive skin with bright green almond-shaped eyes, and dimples on either side of her perfect smile. A lot went on inside her, which she mostly kept to herself. She was popular, smart, and could play any instrument she picked up without a single lesson.

        ✳   ✳   ✳

We moved from Manchester, the biggest city in New Hampshire, to Bedford, New Hampshire—a small town of about twelve thousand people. We lived on a big lot of land—an old farm with a big barn where we would spend our summer days playing. One afternoon, Susie sat us down and told us the story of our brother, Jeffrey. She spoke with the measure and drama of a campfire ghost story.

It was chilling and shocking and tragic, but mostly it was exciting, as most ghost stories are. And like only the best ones, it lived in the front of my mind for a long time after.

✿   ✿   ✿

At this point I was on a tear with the zingers—killing with my parents and sisters, strangers in markets—just being five and saying, "I love tampons!" or any shocking non sequitur was rewarded with "Oh my *gods*" through frenzied laughter. The approval made me dance uncontrollably like Snoopy. The feeling of pride made my arms itch. It fed this tyrant in me that just wanted more more more *push push push*. So when Nana picked us up to go to Weeks' Restaurant for lunch, as she did every Sunday, we got into her big boat, a dark blue Cadillac Seville with a beige leather interior, filled with the odor of stale cigarettes—a smell I loved because it meant "Nana." As all grandkids are to grandmas, we were her world. Before starting the car she bellowed, "Everyone put their seat belts on!" and without a beat I said . . .

(. . . *oh this is going to be <u>GREAT</u>* . . .)

"Yeah—put yer seat belts on—you don't wanna end up like Jeffrey!"

Crickets. No one was even *breathing*. Susie and Laura looked at me with wide, angry eyes. And after several excruciating seconds, Nana broke the silence with an explosion of sobs.

Four words swam in my head—the most grown-up arrangement so far in my five years: *What have I done?*

THE BEDWETTER

Pee Is for "Party"

On August 16, 1977, Elvis Presley saved my life.

The previous afternoon, I played with my six-year-old peers in Heather Peters's backyard. Heather was a towheaded, Aryan dream of perfection. She had one of those pageant moms who resolved that her daughter would be the princess she herself never was. Every other week, Mrs. Peters set Heather's long blond hair in hot curlers, and sent her to school in tight Shirley Temple banana curls. Heather despised this constant humiliation, but I'm sure she understood, as any first grader would, that having your head vandalized is a small price if it can ease Mommy's emptiness. Plus, her father built her this really awesome, gigantic jungle gym.

I was blissfully helping myself to pizza and cake, and to the backyard jungle gym, when Heather asked me where my sleeping bag was. Heather explained—because I had somehow missed, or perhaps willfully ignored—that this party was a sleepover. Fuck me, this is a *sleepover?*

It's helpful to mention, at this point, that I was—and would be for many years to come—a chronic bedwetter. The word "sleepover" to a six-year-old bedwetter has roughly the same impact of, say, "liver cancer" to a forty-year-old alcoholic. The moment the word is spoken, gruesome images of your near-future flood your mind. At least with liver cancer, people gather at your bedside instead of run from it.

I had one reliable means of escaping these situations. I'd explain that I needed my mother's permission to spend the night. I'd call her from somewhere with sufficient privacy, then rejoin my friend with the bad news that my mom wouldn't let me sleep over. But Heather eagerly stood right next to me as I called Mom. Like a hostage with a gun at her temple, I put on an act to satisfy my captor. I "pleaded" with Mom to let me stay over, and, not detecting my insincerity, she granted permission. "Of course, Sweetie. Have fun."

I won't offer much advice in this book, but here's one tip to bedwetters or parents of bedwetters out there: have a code word or phrase. So if your child calls and says, for example, "Your package from Zappos is on its way," or "The man from Moldova wants more lemons," or just "fuzzy dice," you'll know that your child is in danger of pissing herself in someone's house, and you should order her to come home at once.

I hung up the phone, turned to Heather, and harnessed the momentum of my plummeting heart to sling it upward into a joyous, "She said yes!!" It was settled. I would be sleeping in the same living room as Heather and about eight other girls. By this age, I'd peed myself on numerous sleepovers, but here was a chance to do it with a substantial audience.

The anxiety of the impending night took over. I felt like a zombie. Like a paralyzed person in a mobile person's body, going through the motions of a child at play. I didn't bring my own pajamas or linens, so Mrs. Peters provided me a sleeping bag and a pair of Heather's way-too-sexy-for-a-six-year-old pajamas. They were harem-girl bottoms with a short cropped matching top. The anxiety of being in Heather's stuff was stress-gravy on an already terror-filled plate.

As the other girls drifted into their sweet little dreams, I pinched myself awake, constantly testing my bladder. "Do I need to go again? I'll stay up to go one more time . . ." Of course, if you battle against sleep this ferociously, when it finally conquers you, it takes you down hard.

The next morning, I'm the first to wake up. I am warm—which is a trick on people like me. I can stay in denial, lying perfectly still in the warmth, or test it, by moving just the tiniest bit. I venture, rocking my body just slightly to the right. Ice-cold air whooshes along my body and I freeze, heartbroken. I lay, motionless, in panic and urine, for what seems like hours before the other girls start to wake up. I do the only thing a terrified zombie can do: I pretend it didn't happen. I get up with the other girls, take off my PJs like the other girls, and change into my clothes. They are so lucky to be able to move through life so effortlessly. I know at six how lucky they are—they probably still don't know.

Mrs. Peters walks into the room, and before she can say anything, steps right onto the pile of my sexy urine-soaked pajamas. My heart stops as I watch her face burn red like a Disney villainess.

"WHO DID THIS!?!?!" she screams, with a look so scary—like when someone's eyes go wide but with no innocence in them. Just pure fury.

I stand there, quietly enduring the world's youngest heart attack, wishing for my fear to somehow transport me. Am I supposed to answer? Is the onus actually on six-year-old me to fill this silence?

And that's when it happens—Mr. Peters comes in and grabs his wife,

"Elvis Presley died!!!"

The news of the King's death overtook Mrs. Peters, and I was spared. Somehow I got home without the other kids knowing what had happened.

What kind of person reacts to a child's wet pajamas with rage and not compassion? I guess the kind of person who would force hot curlers biweekly on a first grader's head.

Put banana curls on your own head, cunt.

Pee Is for "Partner"

I met Julie Blenkinsop in kindergarten. She had yellow hair and was almost always sucking on her middle two fingers. Her parents were from England. Julie's name was really Julia, but that shit wasn't gonna fly in New Hampshire. Somewhere there's some kind of Ellis Island in New Hampshire (probably in Concord, near the two *New Hampshire Liquor* stores that taunt each other from across the highway), where they look at your name and say,

"Julia?? What ah you, a fuckin' princess? No, youah Julie. If you don't like that you can be Shelly, Dawna, Heathah, o'ah Pam."

The first time Julie slept over at my house, her mother came in to talk privately with mine. When she left, my mother looked at me and smiled. Apparently, Julie had a problem with wetting the bed, and Mrs. Blenkinsop wanted my mother to walk her to the bathroom at some point in the night. This was the greatest news I had gotten in my entire tiny, hairy life. I had my very own partner in shame.

I had no doubt that my chronic bedwetting would be the darkest, most disgrace-filled secret of my life. Only now I had Julie to share it with. Sweet, lovely, finger-sucking, allergy-ridden, rigorously-rubbing-her-nose-with-the-palm-of-her-hand-in-a-circle, Julie.

You Are Getting Very Sleep Pee

At eight years old, my urine showed no promise of abandoning its nightly march out of my urethra and onto my mattress. New Hampshire was running out of clean sheets.

My parents sent me to a hypnotist named Dr. Grimm. Hypnosis was pretty new-agey for New Hampshire, but Julie had been going, and my parents were getting desperate. I had been to doctors before, but all they could offer was a diagnosis of enuresis—meaning my bladder was too small. I was tiny for my age, and with enuresis, there was no medical cure but to grow.

Dr. Grimm was a small bearded man with the kind of gentle voice that sounded suspiciously cultivated. I'd sit on his couch and he'd tell me to close my eyes, and imagine the scenario he described:

"You're walking through a forest and it's peaceful. There are leaves on the ground making a path for you, and you follow it. The sun warms your back. You hear a breeze tapping the leaves of the trees just before you feel it on your face. You can also hear the birds calling to each other on the branches above you, and from a distance, flowing water. You follow the path to a clearing . . ."

What the fuck is a clearing? I'm eight.

" . . . As you come to the clearing you see a stream. You walk to the stream and sit on a rock, welcoming the sun's light . . ."

I was not a cynical person. I was genuinely open to the *idea* of hypnosis. But as he spoke in his affected gentle voice, I could only pretend to be falling under his spell. It was less therapy than experimental theater, with two actors performing a play for no one. I was trying to imagine his path and his forest and whatever a fucking clearing might be, but instead my mind raced, and focused on anything else—the room I was in, the fake calmness in his voice, his beard, the fact that he had a penis and balls. Does doody get on his balls when he poops? Do boys wipe from front to back like girls do? And if so, where does their front start? He can't see what I'm thinking, can he? STREAM! CLEARING! FOREST! DOODY ON HIS BALLS—NO! FUCK! STOP!

Was it my responsibility to let him know his treatment wasn't working? Or was it his to see it? He probably *did* see it, which is weird to think about—that two people can sit in a small room for an hour, fully aware that they are wasting each other's time, but neither will acknowledge it. Anyway, it was back to the piss-and-shame factory that was my bedroom. But at least I had Julie.

Losing Julie

By the end of seventh grade Julie stopped sucking on her fingers, blossomed into a beautiful young woman, and outgrew her enuresis. This all pleasantly coincided with Sarah Wildman's decision to make Julie her new best friend. Sarah Wildman: the most popular girl in school, an effortlessly cool, natural beauty. And all in one day, after eight years of sisterhood, Julie traded up.

This move was not a shallow, heartless, or calculating one. It was a healthy progression for her. In our relationship, I had always been sort of the leader, the alpha female. One day, Julie and I were at our lockers, and though I don't remember what I said to her exactly, her response was, "I'm not going to be bossed around by you anymore!" I was stunned. She was dumping me.

I couldn't even justify being mad. Even then I knew she deserved to hang with the cool crowd. The kind of crowd that wakes up on bone-dry sheets.

While Trying to Prevent My Suicide, My Father Introduces Me to the Concept of Suicide

Unlike Julie, I did not blossom. I didn't grow at all. I was as small in eighth grade as I was in third. Girls were getting tits and periods, and I had seemingly plateaued, elementary-sized. My parents worried, but I also think there was something about me being so small that felt right to us. My dad would always say, "Keep passing the open windows." I didn't know what he meant until he explained that in John Irving's *Hotel New Hampshire*, there's a girl in it who never grows. She becomes a revered novelist but eventually kills herself by jumping out a window. Until then I had never thought of open windows as the opportunities for suicide they truly are.

The following fall was my freshman year of high school. Since Bedford didn't have a high school, I had to take the bus to the big city of Manchester. Manchester High School West was a giant school with thousands of students. I got lost every single day. I didn't know anyone, except for an occasional Bedford kid peppered among the masses. And, you know how there's this giant discrepancy between ninth and twelfth grade?—I mean, Jesus Christ, there were guys with *beards*. There was a fucking *smoking patio*.

I remember one day getting off the bus when Julie, now only a casual friend, spotted me and came over to say hi. She laughed, "Remember how we used to go to that hypnotist for bedwetting? How hilarious was that!?" I laughed and agreed. It *was* hilarious—

though not quite as hilarious as the fact that I was still going to Dr. Grimm. That I was still spending my nights and mornings wishing this humiliating hobby of mine would stop. Not as hilarious as *that*.

Summer Camp:
The Second Worst Kind of Camp for Jews

I realized I was going to be a bedwetter for the rest of my life. I supposed maybe someday this nightmare would end, but even so, you're always an alcoholic, right? Even if you're living dry?

To still be a bedwetter in high school, to have a condition this deeply entrenched, is a pretty serious problem for a child. And to be factually accurate, not every measure my parents took to address the issue was the best one. But to be fair, they were doing what they thought was right. They were loving parents who did the best they could.

One of the biggest—and I would guess most common— mistakes parents make is to transfer their own childhood shit onto their kids. Whatever their joys and agonies were growing up, they assume will be exactly the same for their children, and they let it guide their parenting. I can see the same dumb instincts in myself. When I first started hanging out with my old boyfriend's kids, I found it depressing because I would just look at them and think of how miserable they must be, and how totally alone they must feel. To me, that's what childhood meant. But the truth was they were fine. Happy-go-lucky, even.

When they were kids, my parents were both unhappy during the school year. Both were Jews going to strict and highly religious

Protestant schools in New England, which, in the 1950s, was very much not a blast. In fact, they describe their experiences as "Dickensian." But in the summer Mom and Dad both flourished. They were popular and thrived at their Jewish sleepaway camps, where Dad was hilarious and Mom was a star athlete.

And so, from six years old on, I was sent to sleepaway camp every summer. If you recall from several pages ago the terror I experienced in just one sleepover—now multiply that into a month's worth of nights.

It's not like my parents didn't consider that—they gave my counselors special instructions to walk me to the bathroom in the middle of the night. And let me tell you, the thought of a sixteen-year-old kid knowing my problem was oh so comforting. Summer camp— salvation to both my mom and dad—was, for me, a camp-fiery hell. My teeth were bigger than my face, I was coated in hair, and I smelled like pee. Of course, most events in life are about context. Had my parents instead sent me to live in the Baboon Reserve at the Bronx Zoo, I would have been happy and confident, judging the others for flinging poo, and feeling downright aristocratic.

First there was Camp Conastan. I was six and terrified and knew no one. Laura was there too but she was eleven and I never saw her. I cried every day and wet the bed every night. I would wake up, take off my wet clothes, put them in my hamper bag, and make my cot up like nothing ever happened.

When I was nine it was Camp Huckins. Same scenario, though I made some friends and was great at softball, soccer, and basketball, which gave me some confidence. I was the clown of my bunk, but still, I was sleeping in dried-pee sheets every night, so don't worry about me getting too cocky. I learned to make my bed perfectly after being yelled at in front of the whole bunk by my counselor, Ellen. She said that my hospital corners were shitty (I'm paraphrasing), and as she ripped my bedding apart for me to redo it, a fresh wet circle presented itself in all its glory for the bunk to see. My bunkmates were slack-jawed. Good going, Ellen, you fucking asshole.

When I was eleven I went to a camp called Forevergreen. It was a full eight-week Jewish camp—which was not salvation for me like it was for my parents. I didn't find life in Christian New Hampshire to be a nightmare. I wasn't ostracized for being different (other than being called "gorilla arms"). It was the '80s, not the '50s. This Jewy summer camp wasn't salvation; it was culture shock. Most all the girls had gone there every summer since first grade—they all knew each other, they were all friends.

Keeping a stiff upper lip at Camp Forevergreen

My counselor was the daughter of the people who owned the camp. Her name was Rachel and she was beautiful and blonde (one of those charmed vanilla Jews) and, uncharacteristically for a girl with those characteristics, angry. Superfucking angry. She clearly hated us, hated life, and did not want to be bothered. The perfect candidate to care for children separated from their families for an extended period of time. And who better to be privy to my painful secret, and to be at my side during my nightly marches of shame to the bathroom. She was openly grossed out and annoyed by me.

As I've said, I'm not a cynical person, and I don't believe that human beings are naturally evil. Cuntiness comes from somewhere. In Rachel's case, it was most likely because her sister died of cancer the previous year. For some, that kind of tragedy might make one *more* sensitive to other people's pain. For her, the event either turned her into—or did nothing to lead her away from already being—a cunt. In the middle of the night, with the human tenderness of a morgue technician, Rachel would poke me awake, and with hard, impatient exhales, make sure I knew that this was seriously cutting into her evening plans of sneaking cigarettes and fucking guys.

Another thing about camp: I hated swimming. I couldn't understand how these other kids just jumped into the cold water at swim period. The whistle would blow and all the kids would dive into the lake like little Pavlovian fishies and there I'd be, still on the dock, paralyzed. The counselor would first encourage me to jump in, then *instruct* me to get in, and then finally just scream at me. I'm not sure why I was such a pussy about it, but it was serious to me. The idea of being wet and cold . . . I dreaded swimming in the days as much as I dreaded swimming in my nights.

Life got so bad at Forevergreen that I went a little crazy. I would send letters home saying, "When you get this letter get in the car and pick me up!"

I would pretend that I was in a glass box—that I was in this glass container that no one could see, and it protected me. At night I would open the door and get out of the box to go to bed. In the morning I stepped into it and closed the latch. I dreamed that I would somehow be transported—that all this sadness and fear would actually fuel this glass box and carry me home.

✻   ✻   ✻

Eighth graders at McKelvie School go on a four-day camping trip up Mount Cardigan. I was elected student leader of said camping trip, which I was proud of but extremely nervous and anxious about for a couple of reasons: (1) I was a bedwetter. This is going to be tricky, and (2) did I mention I PISS IN MY SLEEP?!

In the last month of my twelfth year, my mother helped me hide three diapers in the bottom of my sleeping bag and sent me off to go lead my fellow students camping. We were loaded onto the bus and on our way. When we got there, we lifted our gigantic packs onto our backs and up the mountain we hiked, led by me. I don't even think it was an hour before I started sobbing. When the teachers asked why I was crying, I reached for a more stoic answer than the truth.

"I'm worried about my mother being alone without me."

"Aw, I'm sure your mom will be just fine," the teacher said.

"No, she won't! You don't understand," I said, figuring broad and nondescript might be the way to go with this.

As we set up our tents it started to pour, and after eating our smoky, fire-burned dinner, we went to sleep. Surrounded by my tentmates, I subtly reached to the bottom of my sleeping bag with my toes and took care of business without incident, probably because, in their wildest dreams—among the giggling and gossip and talking about boys—they would never guess that one of us was wearing Pampers.

Living with Unrelenting Agony and
Shame Proves to Have a Downside

Our bus pulled into the school parking lot after our long journey. The kids hopped off to be met by their parents. I stepped off the bus and saw my mother, waiting with the other moms, smiling. I was suddenly overwhelmed with shame. I was so embarrassed by my behavior that first day of the trip, and seeing my mother made it real and permanent. This pain was compounded by the fact that with each step of the bus I descended, Mom was snapping pictures of me, the flash illuminating my shame from the inside out. I begged her to stop, but like a shuttering paparazzo she ignored me while continuing to take PICTURES. It's a bizarre way to be ignored.

Here my mom is telling me I'll be happy to have this picture someday.

As I walked to the car, enduring Mom's relentless camera flashes, a wave of . . . something . . . washed over me, and instantly transformed who I was. It happened as fast as a cloud covering the sun. It was at once devastatingly real and terrifyingly intangible. I felt helpless, but not in the familiar bedwetting sense. As quickly and casually as someone catches the flu, I caught depression, and it would last for the next three years.

Another Chronic Condition That Nobody Has Any Fucking Clue How to Treat

Everything about who I was changed. I was not telling jokes. Not chasing laughs. I had always been able to turn pain or discomfort into humor, but that trick was gone now. I couldn't relate to ever knowing it.

I stopped being social. The thought of seeing my friends felt like a burden. All I could focus on was that I was alone in my body. That no one would ever see through the same eyes as me, not ever. It filled me with a loneliness that only deepened when I was not alone.

My friends didn't understand. How could they? I didn't. My parents didn't. My friends even threw a surprise party for me for no reason, thinking it would make me happy again, but all it did was consume me with the guilt of knowing that no party in the world could change the fact that we are all alone.

An Emotionally Disturbed Teenager Is Given a Bottomless Well of Insanely Addictive Drugs As a Means to Improve Her Life, and Other Outstanding Achievements for the New Hampshire Mental Health Community

My parents sent me to a therapist. He was an old man whom my dad had seen give a lecture somewhere about working with kids dealing with divorce. Even though by this point my parents had been divorced for six years, my father figured my sudden depression was most likely a result of it. Who knows, maybe he was right? I walked into the therapist's office, and he had two chairs set up, facing each other. He had me stand with one foot on each chair, explaining that one represented my mother and the other, my dad. As I stood, he pulled the chairs farther and farther apart until I couldn't balance without jumping entirely to one chair or the other.

"I love them both!" I yelped, as I fell forward and off both chairs in defiance.

When Dad picked me up after the session, I told him what had happened, and it was back to the drawing board. The next therapist they sent me to seemed to have more promise. He was a psychiatrist, and that's like a real doctor. I described how I felt and he said, "Sarah, I'm going to write a prescription for a medicine called Xanax, and I want you to take one whenever you feel sad." I was thirteen.

Dr. Riley's office was in a big Victorian house in Manchester, New Hampshire. He shared the house with one other doctor—Dr. Grimm, whom you may recall as the hypnotist who did not manage to hypnotize me.

It was January and pitch-black out already at 4:00 p.m. when my mother dropped me off for my second appointment. I sat in the waiting room and flipped through *People* magazine. By the time I got to the end I realized I had been there for a long time. Finally, movement from upstairs—it was Dr. Grimm. He came down and walked straight to me. As our eyes met I noticed that his were red and tearful. He was trembling. And then, with no elegance, or any sign of bedside manner, he unleashed a primal scream directly into my face: *"DR. RILEY HUNG HIMSELF!!!"*

Following the scream was an ever so slightly more awkward silence. I feel bad that I'm about to make another criticism of Dr. Grimm—he's already come across so poorly in this story—but there is a larger medical point that should be serviced here. There needs to be some protocol, some set of standards, for how we tell depressed teenage girls that their shrinks have killed themselves. I'm not a psychology expert, but it seems to me that screaming the news at them, along with the detail of how it was done, is probably not the way to go. It might be the worst possible way to go. I'm glad that Dr. Riley did not saw off his own head with a chainsaw, or stab himself in the brain by jamming a spoon into his eye socket, because I would *really* not have enjoyed having that primally screamed at me. I'm not saying that Dr. Grimm should have lied to me, or told me that Dr. Riley was carried away by fairies. What I take issue with is the *way* in which he presented the information. At the very least, he might have sat me down and said, "Sarah, there are two kinds of people in the world: those who *don't* prefer to end their own life by strangulation with a rope, and those who do. Dr. Riley, well, he was more the latter."

Like a zombie, Dr. Grimm climbed back upstairs. I sat very still and waited the rest of the hour for my mother to come, my world lit only by the joint efforts of one small reading lamp and one flickering streetlight.

DATE 9/16/85

I'm getting depressed a lot lately. I need to see Dr. Grimmer. Mom made an appointment w/ him for Wednesday. I don't want to be depressed at school! That would be terrible! I just want to

DATE

have the small problems that Jamie and Chip encounter. They seem SO perfect. I'm so scared that I'm losing them! They're my best friends and I don't know what to do w/ out them! Well, I'm getting to bed early tonight. By Sarah Silverman

I Am Diagnosed with Not Having Enough Insanely Addictive Drugs Coursing Through My Veins

My parents took me to another counselor—a registered nurse in Boston whose husband was a doctor. They had a system where she would see patients, diagnose them, and then have big daddy write out the prescriptions. We would make the hour drive up early in the morning and be back by the time school started at 8:00 a.m. She kept me on Xanax but now at regular intervals, instead of just when I "felt bad." I continued not to improve, so each week she upped my dose. By the time I was fourteen, I was taking four Xanax four times a day. Sixteen Xanax per day total.

Although I never said it out loud, in my heart I thought, *This cannot be right*, so I saved each empty prescription bottle in a shoebox in my room as evidence if anything happened to me.

Freshman year of high school I missed three straight months in a row. I just couldn't go to school. I was paralyzed with fear. It was unbearable to be among other kids who were just standing around being fine. It was one of the many inconveniences of this paradox I lived with—the more people I was surrounded by, the more frighteningly alone I felt.

I still did my homework, but instead of my bringing it in, my mother would drop it off. It either speaks well of me, or, more likely, poorly of our public school system, that while attending almost none of my second semester, I maintained a 3.8 grade-point average.

My stepfather, John O'Hara, was the goodest man there was. He was not a man of many words, but of carefully chosen ones. He was the one parent who didn't try to fix me. One night I sat on his lap in his chair by the woodstove, sobbing. He just held me quietly and then asked only, "What does it feel like?" It was the first time I was prompted to articulate it. I thought about it, then said, "I feel homesick." That still feels like the most accurate description—I felt homesick, but I was home.

My stepfather, John O'Hara

Convention Is Upended When a Man with a Porno Mustache Tries to Lure Me INTO a School Yard

Manchester High School West—the school I was not showing up to—was enormous. There were about three thousand students. It was not a bastion of tenderness and attention to individual needs. In my first semester alone, it had chewed up and spit out four freshman math teachers. The fifth one was named Mr. James. He reported for duty on his first day wearing a too-small three-piece brown polyester suit. He had a '70s porn mustache and feathered brown hair. The rumor was that he hadn't even finished high school himself.

After about two months of my not going to school, Mr. James started to show up at my house. My mom and I were actually both shocked that he was even aware of me—I'd been in his class only briefly before I stopped attending, and I was one of, like, 180 students he had. But he came every single day, never invited. We'd sit on the couch and he'd teach me the day's lesson plan, though I could have just as easily taught it to him. For some reason, being with him didn't make me feel alone the way being around other people did. I think because I sensed that maybe he didn't quite fit in this world, either.

Mr. James, his porno/Hitler mustache, and me

After a week of our daily unscheduled meetings, Mr. James asked me to think about returning to school. I said I didn't think I could.

He said, "What about just coming to my class, Period C? It would mean so much to me." He was persistent, and couched it as a favor to *him*. Burdened with the necessity of being polite, I complied. I went just for Period C. Just what he had asked. It wasn't bad. I lived. After that first day I realized, "I could do this." So I went back the next day at Period C, and even stayed through to the end of the day. Within a couple of days, I was back in school full time. My depression was by no means lifted—to the extent that I could feel anything through my regimen of sixteen Xanax per day—but I finished out the year. Thanks to Mr. James.

My Father Tries to Stop the Pee from Coming out of Me but Scares the Shit out of Me Instead

The thing about depression is that, if you're not the one who's actually suffering from it, there's very little you can do to be proactive. If someone in your family is depressed, all you can really do is send them to the shrink, get them their meds, be gentle, and wait. A persistent bedwetting problem, however, is a call to action. Surely there must be a way to stop a small amount of liquid from moving a short distance during a certain time of day. It's a very tangible, physical problem. A science project, really. Combating my depression was a job for an army of geniuses—the ones at Pfizer pharmaceutical company. But the solution to my bedwetting problem, Dad still believed, was within his grasp.

It really killed Dad that I couldn't stop wetting the bed. He was a bedwetter as a kid, too. And, his father, too. Dad was walking me to the bathroom in the middle of the night, but he—understandably—felt it didn't get to the root of the problem. After all,

I was still peeing while sleeping—I was just being escorted to the bathroom to do it. So he started splashing water in my face when he would take me to the bathroom—that way I would be awake and conscious of the motion of *getting up to go.* Though well meaning, this method was both unfruitful and unpleasant.

For a while I had to wear diapers to bed. That way there was no messy changing of the sheets. It was humiliating, but I got used to it. Plus, it *was* convenient. But it was just a Band-Aid, and Dad wasn't about to give up on me.

He put an electric pad under my sheet, designed to set off an alarm when moistened. Though "alarm" doesn't really do it justice, I'd call it more of a shocking, heart-attack-causing, 'Elizabeth, I'm coming to join you' *scream.*

That first night of the screaming aluminum sheet was the last night I slept at my dad's house. I mean, I still spent the night as the joint-custody schedule dictated, but I didn't *sleep.* The horror of waking up to that stunning alarm kept me up most of the night, or until my body couldn't fight it any longer—and you know what happens then—total submission—and all it entails.

More Celebrities Come to My Aid

I stayed up late. I had a TV in my room and I would spend my nights with Johnny Carson and David Letterman. I loved them. Mom loved Johnny—she said, "He's interest*ing* because he's inter-est*ed.*" Also because, she said, "He knows the price of eggs."

One night in 1985, Johnny had an actress on named Jane Badler. Mom perked up, "Ooo ooo! This woman is from New Hampshire!

She was Miss New Hampshire 1972!" We were both so excited to see this pretty lady from New Hampshire on *The Tonight Show*. She was promoting a miniseries she was in, called *V*, in which she played some kind of sexy evil reptile. She was beautiful, and she had black hair like me, which was not common in LL Bean New Hampshire. And then something impossible happened. On Johnny Carson, for everyone in the world to hear, Jane Badler said that when she was a kid she was a bedwetter. This secret that I knew for a FACT would be the most painful secret of my life was a trivial *fun fact* for this elegant, confident beauty queen—actress. Until now, I could not imagine ever getting over the embarrassment of being me, and here she was, giggling about it on *The Tonight Show*. The motherfucking *Tonight Show*.

I Attempt to Make a Career out of Cleaning People's Filthy Sheets but Am Too Depressed to Appreciate the Irony

My father switched me to a different school just before my sophomore year. It was a small college-preparatory school that I got into on the merit of my grades. But by then I had already decided I was going to quit school altogether. Mr. James was heroic and temporarily successful in his efforts to lure me back into school, but it was not enough to conquer my depression or the fear of being alone among a whole new sea of kids.

I secured an interview with the local Sheraton to work there as a maid. The morning before my interview my father pulled up to my mom's house, marched inside, threw me over his shoulder, stuffed me in his car, and drove me to my new school. I screamed and sobbed and tried to jump out of the moving car, but Dad was one step ahead of me, securing the child-safety lock. We pulled into the parking lot of the Derryfield School. Dad got out of the car, came around to the passenger side, and yanked me out as well. Out in the open I was too embarrassed to make a scene. Instead, I used all my will to be tough and choke back tears. I was led into my history class, which was already in progress. The door opened and everyone looked at me. I sat down, concentrating hard on keeping my shit together. I was able for the first time to get out of my own self and focus on my teacher. He was cool and charming and beloved by all students. And he was Jewish! Specifically Russian and Polish, just like me—I couldn't believe it. But most of all he was funny. I never missed another day of school.

There were only about forty kids in my entire grade, and as it turned out, Jim and Sara Riley—the children Dr. Riley was survived by—were students at my new school. Jim was in my grade and Sara was a grade below ours. Though I became good friends with both of them, I never mentioned that I knew their dad, or that I'd seen him a week before his suicide. I wasn't consciously hiding the fact, it just never occurred to me.

While I was settling into Derryfield, I was sent to another shrink, Dr. Santiago (a Mexican doctor in Manchester, New Hampshire—how that happened, I don't know). When I told him I was taking sixteen Xanax a day, he was horrified. He called my mother in and told us that this was fucked-up shit (I'm paraphrasing) and that his very own brother died going off Xanax cold turkey. The weirdest part is that he had been prescribed Xanax for acne. Seriously. He explained that I would go off the Xanax gradually, a half a pill less each week. It was eight months before I was completely off meds—and the day I took that very last swallow of half a Xanax was the happiest day of my life to that point. It was at the bubbler (water fountain) in the hippy dippy hallway of my new school. My shoe-box was to see its last empty bottle.

Relieving Myself

I kept meticulous logs of my bedwetting. I wrote in a diary every night. Each day marked with a "wet" or "dry" in an upper corner. The contents were pretty trivial. "Had a double header against Goffstown. We won the first game 12–6 and lost the second game 7–nothing." Most entries ended the same way, "Bye," then a big swirling "Sarah Silverman."

wouldn't be good for me. I ~~gu~~ guess she was right, but she said that I couldn't ping-pong back and ~~forth~~ to ~~honored~~ houses because it

wasn't fair to ~~them~~. Today was nice. I baby-sat Abby and ~~their~~ this morning ~~until~~ went ~~bonkers~~ w/ Jody. Bye!

2/16/85 —Day—
Today wasn't that great. I was totally depressed all day, (actually from about 3:45–7:20, but it seemed much larger.)

I was so sad and it seemed like no one understood how I felt! When I really thought about it, I think part of the reason that I was upset was

because I feel like such a baby! Especially since Jody is only 3 months older than me and she is almost total self-reliant. And it's not anyone else's fault. I think they treat me my age. It's just me. I don't know what's wrong with me. I'm such a baby. I can't keep myself company. I really need someone w/ me at just about all times and

I kept the "wet" and "dry" logs because I was a detective. (I was in love with Sherlock Holmes—I even had a fingerprinting kit that I used everywhere—proving my mother's use of Tampax or that my sister once held the candy bowl.) I figured keeping the log with my diary might reveal patterns that would help me get to the bottom of this thing. It didn't.

The first thing that actually worked was this kind of chant I made up and I would say to myself, just barely out loud, before bed. I'd kiss my mom or dad goodnight and then shut the door. There is a weird feeling at first, talking out loud when you're alone in a room. But you get used to it:

> *I will not wet the bed.*
> *I will not wet the bed.*
> *I will not wet the bed.*
> *I will not wet the bed.*
> *Do not wet the bed.*
> *Do not wet the bed.*
> *Do not wet the bed.*
> *Do not wet the bed.*
> *Please do not wet the bed.*
> *Please do not wet the bed.*
> *Please do not wet the bed.*
> *Please do not wet the bed.*

I realize now that what kept me dry through those nights weren't my preteen lyrics to this makeshift mantra, but the fact that this was a kind of meditation. Just the fact that I was focusing on one thing for more than a minute, helped. It was probably the intention of the hypnotism with Dr. Grimm, but this thing worked. It was different. It was a prayer.

I finally grew, bladder and all. Around the time that I got my driver's license, and the final traces of Xanax left my system, and the cloud of my depression lifted, my enuresis went away. Just as the doctor had predicted, more than a decade before.

MY NANA WAS GREAT
BUT NOW SHE'S DEAD

My Nana, Rose Silverman, was madly in love with my grandfather Max, which was both pathetic and romantic. Pathetic because she stood by him while he did stuff like belittle my father and punch him in the head, romantic because when she looked at him, all she saw was the man she fell in love with, even when he was cruel, even when he was out of control, even through his many late years of senility.

Nana, still elegant in her later years, and a monkey

Toward the end of his life, Papa would not speak much. When the family came together for dinner, he would look at us with vague recognition and smile. If he opened his mouth at all, it would be to sing one single line of a song—the only thing he seemed to remember from somewhere in the recesses of his mind, *"And he'll be big and strong, the man I love . . ."*

"That's a song for a woman to sing, Mac!" my Nana would yell, lovingly. To be fair to Papa, the lyrics were written by Ira Gershwin, who by all accounts was a man.

Even though I felt protective of my dad, who was mentally and physically abused—directly at the hands of Papa and indirectly by Nana's unconscionable passivity—I couldn't help but adore my Nana. She wasn't the same person with me as she had been with Dad so many years before. It seems to me that sometimes the worst parents make the best grandparents. I'm not sure why. Maybe because there is enough of a generational separation that they don't see their grandchildren as an extension of themselves, so their relationship isn't tainted by any self-loathing. And of course, just growing older seems to soften and relax people. Since so many people these days don't seem to start their families until around age forty, I predict there will be less child beating, but more slipped disks from lifting babies out of cribs. Even the father of advanced age who's not inclined to spare the rod is likely to suffer more than his victim: The first punch he throws might well be the last straw for his rotator cuff, reducing his disciplinary options to mere verbal abuse and napping. I'm excited about the next generation!

Nana was social but she wasn't quite a woman of the world. Her Catholic neighbor once invited her over for drinks, and on the wall Nana noticed a picture of a woman holding a baby.

"Is this you and your mother?" she asked.

She genuinely didn't know from the Madonna and Child, but then again, Jews don't tend to view biblical iconography as a foundation for home decor. In their houses, those spaces are reserved for flocked silver wallpaper and refrigerator magnet pictures of grandchildren.

When my sisters and I would walk into the room, Nana's face lit up like a kid on Christmas morning. (I couldn't think of the Jewish equivalent analogy other than "like a Jewish woman seeing her grandchildren . . .")

Rose and Max Silverman—Nana and Papa—walking down the aisle at my parents' wedding, during the very short-lived heyday of Jews in top hats

Nana was elegant and ladylike and fashionable. She was also hysterically funny. She knew all the dirtiest jokes and used them as bargaining chits with me—if I behaved well or did this chore or that, I would be rewarded with a joke. "Everyone was feeling Rosie, so Rosie went home. Then they all jumped for Joy!" Though she was stuck in old-time notions of right and wrong, she tried to be progressive around us. Anytime we would tell her about a new boy in our lives, she'd ask,

"Is he Jewish?"

"No, Nana, he's not."

"Oh." Then, remembering herself, "Well . . . is he nice?"

She would say nonsensical things that not only made complete sense to her, but were vital and required immediate heeding. For example, as we were leaving her house after a visit, she'd often yell after us, "Don't get a perm!"

Only two liquids passed her lips: black coffee and Manhattans. I guess nothing was worth ingesting unless it carried some powerful psychoactive agent. Manhattans, of course, are just enormous helpings of pure whiskey. One of them should have easily toppled a woman of Nana's age and size, but she usually maintained pretty well. Although I do recall once, after dining out at a restaurant that served especially generous drinks, a vision of Nana singing "Give My Regaahhds to Broadway" through bouts of hysterical laughter, as she tripped out of the car and up the stone steps to her house.

She told stories that led seemingly nowhere:

"I was watching Rosie [O'Donnell's daytime talk show], and she had an actress on . . ."

And just when you think this was going somewhere, she'd put her hand on my arm and say (in her thick New Hampshire accent), simply,

"You-ah pretty-ah."

That was the peculiar thing about Nana's love—while most Jewish grandmothers have an astronomically inflated view of their grandchildren's wonderfulness, hers was uniquely realistic. She often said, "To *me*, you are so wonderful. To *me*, you are so beautiful." I suppose there's a number of ways to interpret that: (a) she was hedging, uncertain that, empirically, I was beautiful or wonderful, and wanted to speak with legal precision, should she someday be accused of misleading me; (b) she wanted to give me love, but didn't want me to get a fat head about it; (c) she wanted a little extra credit for being bold and brave and enough of a visionary to stand alone—the *only* one to perceive how beautiful and wonderful I was.

Peculiar rhetoric aside, Nana would always be hopelessly and blindly devoted to her granddaughters.

My father once got a call from Carlyle House, the nursing home where Nana eventually settled. They said she was being rushed to the hospital. He raced over there so he could ride in the ambulance with her, and when he ran through the hall to her room, she was already being rolled out on a gurney by two male EMTs. She looked up at the men, pointed to my dad, and said, "That's the fathah of the girls I was telling you about."

When it became clear that Nana was dying, my sisters and I came home to New Hampshire to be with her. She would wake up in between long periods of sleep and ask if she was still alive. When we told her she was, she would slap her hand on her head as if a waiter had just fucked up her cocktail order for the ninth time in a row. I always figured that when you die of old age, you just go when you're ready. Nana was ready to go but she wasn't . . . going. It was torture to watch her waiting so impatiently to get the fuck out of this world. But still she was funny. At the end, as Laura and I sat on either side of her, each holding one of her hands, Nana came to, briefly. She looked up at us, smiled, and whispered, "So beautiful."

Laura jumped right in saying, "She's talking to me!"

I said, "No way, she's talking to me!"

To which Nana, with what was literally one of her last dying breaths, replied, "Laura."

HYMEN, GOODBYEMEN

I Find That Sex Agrees with Me

I did some bad things.

Not "bad things" like murder or rob. But there was a period in which I couldn't see a guy without needing to know what his balls looked like. Between 1990 and '92, I tore through New York City like the Tasmanian Devil. I use the Tasmanian Devil metaphor with some hesitation because, though I like it for the visual image, it's imperfect. The Tasmanian Devil from the Warner Bros. cartoons was this explosion of frustrated energy that rampaged unstoppably, but one gets the sense that if he ever got laid, he would relax and turn into someone with whom you could conceivably get stoned. In the early '90s, sex didn't do that for me. It didn't especially calm me down or satisfy me, it was just something I did in between all the other times I was having sex. Additionally, the Tasmanian Devil is slightly hairier than I was then. Ever so slightly . . .

Anyway, my point is that I had some sex in my early twenties. In part, I was making up for lost time. I was a late bloomer all around. My period came late, my ability not to go off like a fucking lawn sprinkler every night came late, and sex came late. Essentially, everything having to do with the general flow of traffic in my vagina came late. Ironically, I was this girl in high school through whom everyone came to learn about sex, though I, myself, had never gone past kissing a boy.

My first real love was a girl named Kerry.

The Adventures of the Dirty Jew
and the Nigerian Princess

I met Kerry in my sophomore year in high school. I was a scrub in blue-and-green-plaid flannel pajamas, which I wore to school every day and slept in every night. (But to be clear, I had pretty much stopped wetting the bed by then, plus I showered and changed my underwear daily. Not that I needed to, as I was still at a prepubescent stage in which I genuinely incurred no gaminess.) Kerry was my age, but she was a full-grown woman. She had long painted fingernails, she read fashion magazines, and she went to the gym—what high school kid goes to the fucking gym? She even used eye cream at night. "You can never start too early," she'd say.

She was my best friend and I worshipped her.

When I refer to "love," I mean an intense, profoundly meaningful, somewhat-exclusive-in-nature relationship with a peer, which radically shaped me. If you're expecting to read about me engaging in teenage exotic lesbian sex, you may be disappointed—or perhaps relieved. I wish I had a story for you like that. But I just don't—and never did—have an interest in vaginas, other than for their comedic value.

As different as Kerry and I were, we were peas in a pod. My guess is because we were the black and the Jew in a sea of whiter-than-white preppy rich kids, and both from bleeding-heart liberal homes in a district of conservatives.

Kerry spoiled me like a grandmother. She would come to school armed with gifts for me. "Here, Sarah. I bought you some candy on my way to the gym." To her, I was a puppy that needed grooming. On my seventeenth birthday she gave me a shoebox labeled "Zit Kit," filled with all the soaps and creams she felt would work best with my skin. She would give me tips, like "Don't touch your face. It clogs your pores." When I slept over at her house, she would read aloud to me from the likes of the fashion magazine *Elle*, and the Linda Lovelace sex-slave autobiography, *Ordeal*.

Kerry was adopted. Half black and half white, she had learned her biological parents were a red-headed French woman and a Nigerian prince who met as transfer students in Ohio. Her adoptive parents were white granola-headed feminist hippies, which didn't make sense at all. Though maybe it's why she loved white, granola-headed me.

Kerry and me junior year of high school

Kerry could talk her way out of anything. She would find us days off from school no one else had. She would march to the principal's office and explain, "I am exploring Judaism and tomorrow is Tu Bishvat. Sarah and I will be missing the school day in order to properly celebrate this most precious of days." We would get in her car and just go. Usually to Boston, usually with weed procured, and usually in Kerry-sanctioned outfits inappropriate for school or temple. Such outfits would include tight black jeans, high heels, hoop earrings (all borrowed from Kerry), big hair, black eyeliner with sparkled silver eyeliner *liner,* and fitted tops with just a promise of cleavage.

Kerry, Nubian princess

I co-opted Kerry's sexy confidence, but it was a chemical compound that combusted when combined with my aggressive juvenility.

I would walk the halls carrying my sixty pounds of private-school hardcovers, and if I saw the headmaster, Mr. Hurlbut, I would just throw them all up in the air and collapse on the floor in a dramatic flourish.

"Sarah! Pick that up!"

"What? I fell! You can't yell at me for *falling*."

I swear to God I wouldn't have done shit like that if I didn't know deep down, that, for whatever reason, he loved it. It was a subtle kind of domination. It got to the point where, when he would see me in the hall with all my books in tow, he would plead with me,

"Sarah, don't . . ."

Delighted, I would sway, back and forth, like I was balancing on a ship in rough waters—

"Whoooooaaaaaa."

"Sarah—please . . ."

"Losing . . . balance . . ."

Sometimes I'd explode, books and papers everywhere (my own books and papers, that I'd have to then clean up, but totally worth it to me). Sometimes I'd let him off the hook, finding my balance and moving past. Two ships.

Junior year I lost my license for three months for going 90 in a 55, then pulling over to the *left* side of the five-lane highway when stopped by the state trooper. For three months, Kerry picked me up every day before school. First we'd get some french toast sticks at Burger King, then we'd go to the parking lot and she'd give me a lesson on how to drive a stick shift, then to school. She said every woman should know how to drive a stick.

Kerry could make my day or break my heart. She would sometimes leave me waiting for hours. Sometimes she wouldn't show up at all. But she was unscoldable. I was too in awe. It's the memory of this feeling, of this dynamic, that makes me call her my first love.

Ordinary friendships don't have these capabilities. The intensity of our relationship didn't allow room for boyfriends anyway.

I was fiercely loyal and protective of Kerry. Once we went to the twenty-four-hour bowling alley in Manchester. I got my shoes and went to our assigned lane to put them on. I looked up and Kerry was bolting toward me, furious and hurt. She sat down and said,

"The guy gave me the shoes and said, 'Make sure you wear socks with these, you dirty nigger.'"

Before she even finished the word I was flying at the clerk in what I believe was murderous rage. And in the moment just before I got to him, Kerry screamed to me, "I'm kidding! Sarah—I'm kidding!!" I looked back and she was laughing hysterically. I don't know why she did that. I don't know if it was really a joke as much as maybe a test of some kind, but I was so relieved, firstly because of the hate it would so glaringly imply, but mostly because I didn't know what I was gonna do when I got to that fucking shoe stand.

After high school Kerry dropped in and out of my life at her whim, like a fairy godmother I couldn't summon but who came when she felt I needed her. (She still does.)

Like in Every Young Girl's Dream, My Delicate Flower Is Taken by a Gruff Thirty-Year-Old Comic from Queens Who Is Emotionally Indifferent to Me

---

Kevin Brennan was the emcee on open-mike nights, Mondays, at the Boston Comedy Club on West 3rd Street in the West Village of Manhattan. I had a job passing out flyers for the club every Thursday, Friday, and Saturday from 4:00 p.m. to 2:00 a.m., and besides my ten-dollars-an-hour payment, I could go up on open-mike night without bringing two friends (a prerequisite for open-mikers was that they had to bring two paying customers).

Kevin was tall with dark brown hair and a white-and-red blotchy Irish face. He wore a long army green trench coat and carried a briefcase, which, at nineteen, I found very impressive. And he was thirty—a grown man. He stood outside the club smoking a Merit Light. I went outside and bummed one.

KEVIN: *So, you go to school?*

ME: *Yeah. NYU.*

KEVIN: *What—are you a freshman?*

ME: *Mm-hm.*

KEVIN: *What—are you, like, in a sorority?*

ME: *Yeah, but you can only be in it if you're really cool.*

KEVIN: *Yeah? Who else is in it?*

ME: *Just me.*

He laughs.

Let me take a moment to describe myself here: big curly perm, black polyester shirt with long shear sleeves, black miniskirt, and Doc Martens with thick black socks. It was 1990.

I did my five minutes and stayed for the rest of the night until the show was over and Kevin was going home.

"You wanna see my apartment?" He chuckled, I assume at his paper-thinly veiled offer. "It's in Queens."

"Sure. Yeah."

And off we cabbed to Astoria, Queens. We walked up a stairwell and through a hallway to his apartment. It smelled good to me. It smelled like first grade for some reason. Something industrial but sweet, like old paint and licorice. Inside there was a small living room, a bathroom, and two bedrooms—one his and one his roommate's. On the coffee table was a *Best of Chicago* tape. He also had a stack of records, with the Go-Go's *Vacation* on top.

"Wanna see my bedroom?"

"Okay."

He led me to his bedroom—a bed, a dresser, and an ashtray. He kissed me while he laid me back in his bed.

"Have you ever had sex before?"

"Yes, I've had sex before," I said, insulted.

Here's the thing. I thought I *had* had sex. My senior year of high school I visited my sister Laura at Boston University, and she fixed me up with a friend who was from all accounts very good-looking. I knew he was the kind of guy girls in my school would think was really hot. He was in college; he was tall and lean and had long hair and a long beard—like a sexy Jesus. We sat on my sister's tiny living room couch and watched *Dead Ringers*, a creepy Jeremy-Irons-as-twin-gynecologists thriller and fell asleep before anything really serious happened. The next morning my sister and her roommate left early for the AIDS Walk, and this guy and I—yipes, I can't remember his name, maybe Brooks or something like that—moved into my sister's bedroom. He put on a condom and pushed against me, but there was honestly no hole there. I figured that was it. The guy just pokes hard between your legs for a while. Sex. When he finally gave up, he said, "It's not like it is in the movies, Sarah. Is that what you thought?" Which was a weird thing to say right after watching *Dead Ringers*.

"No," I said defensively.

So when Kevin asked me if I was a virgin, I answered honestly: No. Somehow I think he knew better than me, because he pretty much instructed me through the whole process. He talked me through my first blowjob (that, I admitted I had never done before), what to do with my tongue, what not to do with my teeth, and so on. And then, slowly at first, he pushed inside me. All the way inside. And all I could think was,

Holy shit, THIS is sex, Dummy.

He sat up on the side of the bed to smoke another Merit Light, carefully ridding the end of any excess ash, molding the red tip of it into a constant point. He put out his cigarette and pulled back the sheets to get up, revealing a Rorschach-like pattern of blood. Like a red butterfly stamp, getting lighter and lighter with each imprint.

There was a long moment of silence before I worked up the moxie to say,

"That came out of you."

"Um. No it didn't."

Another long pause, broken by him,

"It's okay. Just buy me new sheets."

I Make the Highly Original Choice of Falling for a Guy Who Treats Me Poorly

Kevin didn't have much time for me, but I took whatever I could get. I couldn't wait to have sex again and again and again. It was awesome. I was in love.

The feeling wasn't mutual. As it turned out, there's a reason thirty-year-olds sleep with nineteen-year-olds, and it's not because they're looking for something real. I beautified myself in my dorm room, checking the time and myself alternately all night for a date with him that never happened, and when I saw him next and accused him of sleeping with someone else that night, he just said, "It wasn't my fault she tricked me," with an *I don't give a fuck* half-smile.

After six months of being his if-he-couldn't-find-anyone-better fallback sex, I gave him a letter with the ultimatum that he had to be nicer to me or it was over. He opened it immediately and read it in front of me, laughing, "Then I guess it's over."

Not long after that Kerry came to visit from Washington. Her hair now dreaded and multicolored, she told me all about Howard University and her life in D.C., i.e.,

"Crackheads are the best because you can get your whole lawn mowed for, like, two dollars."

She asked me how I was and I told her that I lost my virginity but the guy dumped me and I was devastated.

"Fuck that shit. I'm a female chauvinist."

"Um . . . huh?"

"I'm a female chauvinist. I tell a guy, 'When I'm with you I'm with you, and when I'm not with you, you don't worry about where I am.' "

I was inspired. Kerry changed my perspective—changed the way I saw men and changed the way I saw myself, transforming me from prey to predator in one weekend visit. For the next two years I was on a rampage. I was a monkey swinging from vine to vine. I kept Noxzema in my bag because I never knew where I'd end up sleeping or whom with. (Book of Kerry: Never go to sleep with a dirty face.)

The following is a conversation between Kevin and me while I was writing this. I got in touch to make sure it was okay with him and to find out what he remembered.

----- **Original Message** -----

From: Sarah Silverman
To: Kevin Brennan
Sent: Tue, 10 Feb 2009 9:00 pm
Subject: Sarah Silverman

Alright, Kevin. Tell me about that night as well as you remember it. Unless you don't want to.
Do you want to? Do you even remember?
Whatever you can recall I'd appreciate.

I'm Jewish,
S

----- **Original Message** -----

From: Kevin Brennan
To: Sarah Silverman
Sent: Wed, 11 Feb 2009 3:38 pm
Subject: Got your message

Yes, I remember that night because when you became famous people would ask me about it so I would reminisce. The best part was after I asked you if you were a virgin because there was blood on the sheets and your response was "maybe it's your blood." Then I knew you were a virgin because guys don't bleed after sex (unless you're Mario Cantone, etc) and you would have known that if you had gotten laid before.

From: Sarah Silverman

To: Kevin Brennan
Sent: Wed, 11 Feb 2009 6:08 pm
Subject: Re: Got your message

I don't think you told me to buy you new sheets, but it seemed like a good ending, and though this is nonfiction, I decided it was completely in your character to do so. You did, after all, jump behind me to protect yourself. Remember? I got hit by a van that just barely stopped in time.

Why is that "Wind Beneath My Wings" song suddenly in my head?

xo
sarah

From: Kevin Brennan

To: Sarah Silverman
Sent: Thu, 12 Feb 2009 10:14 pm
Subject: Re: Got your message

Your version makes me sound cool and pathetic at the same time like that guy who scalps tickets in Fast Times at Ridgemont High. Whatever happened to him? Also, the van didn't hit you, it only came close. And I only did it because I was taping MTV 1/2 Hour comedy hour that week so my life was more valuable than yours.

From: Sarah Silverman

To: Kevin Brennan
Sent: Thu, 12 Feb 2009 10:28 pm
Subject: Re: Got your message

Touche.
Xo
s

ps—do you wipe shit out of your baby's asshole?
pps—It's *her* shit in there, right? That would be gross otherwise.

SOME OF MY MORE MOVING VIOLATIONS

I've never been raped. Let me rephrase: At 5:38 p.m. on December 17, 2009, as I'm writing this chapter, I have not up to this point ever been raped. But then again, in my youth, there were certain key incidents during which I was treated with such cruel and reckless abandon by the males involved that, technically speaking, I probably have been 10 to 12 percent raped. There were terrifying moments in which rage-fueled assailants physically overpowered me, inflicting deliberate, prolonged, and gleeful torture, while making me fear for my life. These are the kind of moments that, decades later, still haunt my dreams, so I thought it would be fun to share them with you.

Prelude: My Extremely, Extremely Brief Relationship with a Domestic Turkey

---

We lived on a farm, but it wasn't operational like our neighbors' farms, which produced stuff; we bought our meat and vegetables from them. When I was six years old, my dad took me there to see the turkeys. The farmer, Vic, told me to look at all the birds carefully and choose one that I liked. I saw a cute one with a silly walk and said, "Him!!" Before my pointing finger dropped back down to my side, Vic had grabbed the bird by the neck and slit his throat. Blood sprayed as the turkey's wings flapped back and forth in a futile attempt to unkill itself. Without realizing it, I had sentenced that turkey to death, and while maybe this sort of thing gave fat British monarchs a rush, to me it was horrifying. And though I'm probably projecting, I don't think it was in the turkey's top-five favorite moments, either.

I should mention that this was late November, so what I had witnessed was not random cruelty, but a long-standing American tradition. This wasn't just a random turkey killing, it was a *thankful* turkey killing. Until that day I didn't even know where meat came from, so if that trip to the farm was Dad's deliberate attempt to teach me about the food chain, I wish he'd used a tad more finesse. My parents taught me about where babies come from, but they didn't exactly force me to watch while my father bent my mother over the kitchen table. I'm not saying that children should be shielded from the facts of life, just that six-year-olds don't need them demonstrated in such visual detail.

In hindsight, I'm sure my dad feels bad about our little excursion, but I see it as a gift. My father might not have realized or intended it, but that day he gave me the knowledge to make an informed decision for myself at a very early age: I would never eat turkey again. And once I figured out the connection between Happy Meals and cows, I would never eat beef again, either. Or any other meat.

Adam Gillan Enters My Life and Mouth

I didn't exactly make a big deal about my vegetarianism. In my town, people didn't really understand it, and I figured that bringing it up would only cause trouble. But somehow, sophomore year, Adam Gillan found out.

Adam was a bully. He was also tall, strong, handsome, popular, charismatic, funny, and a brilliant athlete who engaged in many extracurricular activities. And while I don't think there was a specific school-sponsored club for it, he excelled at preying on the vulnerable. He was a bully in that '80s teen-movie way, the kind who would have been torturing Jon Cryer.

When Adam discovered that I was a vegetarian, it rocked his world. He couldn't get his head around it. To see his enraged reaction you would've guessed he'd just found out someone had stuck his mother with an AIDS-infected needle. Instead, someone would have had to correct you: "No, Mrs. Gillan's fine. This is much, much worse—he just found out the Jew doesn't eat Big Macs."

I was sitting alone in the empty cafeteria doing homework when Adam and his two minions, J.R. and Gade, approached. Gade was a curly, towheaded sheep, while J.R. was a short musclehead with a mullet who bragged about how his biceps were getting so big that he couldn't comfortably put his bulging arms down at his sides. (It was an impressive handicap, although not quite as impressive as his worldview—expressed to me like a father giving advice to his son—that all women were whores and all men whoremasters.)

When I looked up, J.R. and Gade were standing over me, giddiness etched on their faces. I had noticed this expression on boys at least once before when I was at soccer practice—just before they came toward me, threw me down, and rubbed my forearm hair really hard as if they were trying to make glass out of sand, although in fact they were making tiny knots that my mom had to cut off with tiny sewing scissors. I didn't cry during that attack; more than anything, I was amazed that my arms could do that.

So when I spotted that familiar glint in the eyes of Adam and his sidekicks, I thought, *What is this gonna be?* It was this: While Adam stood by, clutching a heaping stack of cold cuts from the cafeteria, Gade and J.R. held me down on the cafeteria table, arms pinned and outstretched like another Jew you may or may not know, and J.R. clamped my nose shut with his free hand. Then they waited patiently, giggling, for my body's breathing instinct to force my mouth open. At which point, Adam, not missing a beat, stuffed the cold cuts inside. I gagged at the taste and smell, simultaneously gasping for air through the blockade of highly processed dead-animal flesh. By now it had been seven full years since I'd last tasted meat. To call this event unpleasant would be something of an understatement.

There was no point in telling on him; it would only cause trouble for me. And since no rape kits had been designed to prove oral penetration by cold cuts—suddenly the phrase "hide the salami" had a whole new meaning—I wasn't sure that anyone would believe me anyway.

I wonder if that experience was as satisfying for Adam as it was traumatizing for me. What had he hoped to accomplish? If he wanted to teach a dumb vegetarian a lesson, it failed. I did not, after that encounter, say to myself, *Well, message received: Meat is appetizing, and it's time to put this childish vegetarian thing behind me.* If anything, my negative attitude toward eating meat deepened. If he really wanted to teach me a lesson, he should have found a child suffering from severe malnutrition, specifically from protein and iron deficiencies, and forced me to expound upon my bourgeois dietary politics to the starving child's face. Now, that could have been life changing. I guess what I'm saying is, if you need to be a bully because you tremble with all that pent-up hostility and aggression, try being clever about it.

"Hanging Out" with Sandy

I went to visit my sister Laura in Berkeley, where she was attending summer school. I was then thirteen and so *tiny* that I looked like a nine-year-old. And in those days our food supply wasn't being pumped with hormones or whatever it is that seems to produce the enormous breasts, densely vegetated mons pubis, and full-tilt ovulation that even some ten-year-old girls enjoy today.

The Berkeley trip offered many new experiences. I'd never flown by myself, and this was my first time seeing California. But most exhilarating was the complete freedom that came with zero adult supervision. My sister was in class all day, so I wandered around Berkeley on my own. I'd stumble onto pick-up soccer games and jump right in. I took myself to lunch at this place called Blondie's—it sold the biggest slice of pizza I'd ever seen—and stared at girls who had hot pink hair, or rats living on their shoulders.

Laura's dorm was co-ed, and her next-door neighbor was a boy named Sandy. He had blond, shoulder-length hair and what seemed to be zero classes to go to, so he was available to hang out with me all day. Even though Sandy was eighteen, he took a surprising amount of interest in teeny, tiny, thirteen-year-old me. Another thing Sandy took a great interest in was drugs, though I didn't quite put it together at the time. I would wake up well after Laura had left for class, put on shorts and a T-shirt, and knock on Sandy's door. He would always be chilled out, and always welcomed me in. To a degree, I can now relate; little kids *are* funny when you're stoned.

One day, though, the chilled-out Sandy had been replaced by a manic, crazy-eyed look-alike who opened the door and shooed me inside, with an energy that made me sense something was off. I plopped down on the floor as he closed the door behind me, and just as I felt the wind coming through the open window, he picked me up, carried me to its edge, and hoisted me out by the ankles—dangling my body headfirst twelve stories above the ground. I still have no idea what instigated this. We weren't in the midst of an argument, I didn't owe him a large sum of money, and as far as I know neither of us had been thinking, *I wonder what it's like to be suddenly faced with one's own mortality?* It just happened so fast. I'd been sitting on the floor, and the next thing I knew I was staring at cars and people who looked like tiny dots far below me, and feeling a totally unfamiliar anxiety about the condition of the ligaments that connected my ankles to my tibias. I was startled by a loud, bloodcurdling noise, before I realized it was coming from me. I was screaming like, well, like a child dangling upside down from the twelfth floor of a seventeen-story building.

It is, to say the least, weird to be held in such a position from such a height, because your potential murderer also happens to be the only person who can save your life. You might say the same thing of someone who's holding a gun to your head, but there's an important difference: That person must make a conscious effort to blow your brains out and a conscious effort to pull the trigger, while the person dangling you out the window only needs to *stop* making an effort. It's a very passive kind of killing. Human nature being what it is, I'm far more worried about the likelihood of murder being triggered by laziness, inertia, or any other expression of giving up.

Sandy instructed me to continue screaming, not that I needed prompting—especially once he'd explained that until I had "screamed enough" he couldn't bring me inside. "Enough" is a little subjective, but naturally I did my best. Trying to guess at just how much was enough would have been challenging even without my head close to bursting with blood.

At some point Sandy got whatever his definition of what "enough" was and pulled me back in. I'd like to think it was because of some sort of negotiating skill on my part, something that could serve as a template for future situations in later life, but it wasn't. Screaming *"AAAAGGHH!!!!"* has never since gotten me anywhere.

The kind of horseshit he had pulled probably happens to kids all the time, and it's a bummer. Whatever mistakes my parents made, they always *tried* not to damage me. They never hit me; they encouraged me, and gave me love in the best way they knew how, and when I suffered, they worried, tried to help, and took me to doctors. And still, just by leaving the house, I could get gang-assaulted on a cafeteria tabletop and dangled out a fucking twelfth-story window by some drugged-out psychopath. I'm just saying, it's a kick in the pants, you know?

On the day I returned home to New Hampshire, Sandy gave me a going-away present (one, that is, in addition to a brush-with-death sore throat). He handed me a brown paper bag and said, "Don't open this until you get on the plane." So on that plane, in the middle seat sandwiched between two businessmen, I opened my gift: one *Playgirl* magazine, two *Penthouse Forums*, and a *Cheri*. I can say with some confidence that this gift turned out to have a fair amount of influence on my life. At least it fed my fascination with sex, which in turn informed some of my earlier work, as seen below, in a self-penned *Penthouse Forum* letter.

—Someone asked me what I wanted to do —I said well or
— In Letter form — PoV of young man new to LA   for the

Dear Penthouse Forum;

I used to think that these letters were made up by your
writing staff, but after my last trip to LA--boy did I change
my tune! I went to "The Viper Room'" (Famed by owner Johnny
Depp and the untimely death of River Phoenix,) and had the
time of my life. I wasn't dancing much because I'm shy and
have two left feet. I was watching people party on the dance
floor when one woman in particular seperated herself from
the crowd and started to give my her own private show. ~~This
woman was no dog, she was a fucking lioness.~~ She had a
long mane of fire red hair and huge titties that had a dance
all their own with each subtle movement of her sensual slink.
    "I've never seen you here before." she said,
I was trying so hard to be cool. "That's because I usually
hang at House of Blues." Her face lit up with excitment,
I had obviously scored big points with the Ackroyd ref.
I could see her nipples get hard under her tight spandex
~~blouse.~~
    "Do you like to fuck dirty?" I wasn't sure what she meant
exactly, but I definately wanted in. I started to reply,
but she cut me off.
X   ["Your a dirty birdy aren't you. I like dirty fucking
birdies.] Meet me in the bathroom in five minutes." &Off
she went toard the bathroom, leaving me rock hard, and making
five minutes seem like a fucking eternity.
    Finally it was time to make my move. I walked into the
bathroom, and lo and behold, there she was. As soon as I
walked in, she locked the door , so as not to be disturbed.
It didn't take a genius to realize she's done this before.
    "I'm gonna suck your sweet Man-ass." she said. And before
I knew it she was at my waist licking away. I had never
experienced a rimmer before. and I had never realized how
pleasurable it could be. Then in one swift movement she swept
her luscious tongue across my balls and engulfed my rock
hard cock. It took all the restraint I could muster not
to blow my chunky load down her wet suck-pump.
    After a few minutes she (GOT JEANS) stopped. My pussy's getting
jealous of my mouth. And with that she sat down hard on my ~~~~~~~~
my ~~Italian sausage.~~ log.   Sweet !! .

This is
the denoument

"I'm coming!" She screamed. At this point I exploded inside her, pulled out and shot the rest of my cheese on her sweet tits.

It's a good thing we were finally done because by this time people were pounding on the door to use the can.

I never caught your name." I said, as we quickly dressed.

"Debbie Schwarts." She said, her husky voice now seeming more like a grating whine.

"That sounds like a jewish name." I *laughed*.

"It is." She said. This was no joke. I had just fucked a *god damn* a jew!

Well, I guess the joke was on me. I still brag to my friends about my adventure at the Viper Room, but I just leave out the Jew part.

Earl Waterman
Ithaca,NY

SARAH SILVERMAN: THE COLLEGE YEAR

I Wait Until Third Grade to Make Major Life Decisions

In third grade, the teacher gave us questionnaires that asked what we wanted to be when we grew up. I wrote, "A comedian, an actor, or a masseuse." Like Mozart, my destiny was evident at a very young age, and it would be only a brief twenty-five years later that I would get my own television show. Another way in which Mozart was like me: I'm pretty sure he thought farts were hilarious. If I could travel back in time and have lunch with him, I bet he and I would have loads to talk about. Can you imagine the scene? When I reach the Steve Martin-y phase of my career, I'll write a play about such an encounter. The question is, Will I go see it? In all likelihood I will sincerely intend to but will wind up at home instead, watching some future version of *Lost*, should one exist.

I Develop My Act and Breasts, in That Order

Between junior and senior years of high school, I went to Boston University summer school, and one night I decided to check out

Stitches Comedy Club on Commonwealth Avenue. I'd never been inside a comedy club before, and I was underage, but somehow I weaseled my way in. As I entered, I heard a woman's voice on the mike. It was Wendy Liebman, who at the time was an emerging talent but would go on to become a major comic. Through her signature strained smile, she said, "Somebody told me I looked like Ruth Buzzi today. I don't know who she is—is she pretty?" Each joke that followed was funnier than the one before it. I was blown away. I found out when the next open mike was and signed myself up.

Although it would be my first real open mike, I was not especially nervous. It might be that I'm one of those people who are naturally comfortable on a stage. Besides, I'd had some practice telling jokes in front of an audience. My high school had assemblies on Mondays and Fridays, and, hippie school that it was, there was always extra time for kids to get up and make an announcement or, in my case, tell a couple jokes. But maybe my lack of stage fright was the upside of years of nightly bedwetting. Maybe that daily shame had ground away at my psyche, like glaciers against the coastline, so that somewhere in my consciousness, I understood that bombing on stage could never be as humiliating. My early trauma was a gift, it turned out, in a vocation where your best headspace is feeling that you have nothing to lose.

My set was pretty successful. I told some jokes about high school and ended the gig with a song about being flat-chested, which at the time I was. Soon, though, I did develop breasts. Fairly substantial ones. But I was slow to realize I needed to adjust my act. It wasn't until I moved to New York and started doing stand-up that Kevin Brennan told me so eloquently, "That song isn't funny because you have tits." This moment marked the end of a three-year high school epoch characterized by wisecracks such as, "Hey, Sarah! I just heard a joke that will blow your tits off! Oh, you already heard it."

I was so excited after my first open mike that I couldn't wait to do it again. But I still had to finish high school, and there wasn't much of a comedy scene in Manchester, New Hampshire. But there was a place called La Cantina where bands performed, and when I asked if I could open for one of them with my stand-up, the owner said yes. That night there was a table packed with drunk people in the back, and whenever I would deliver a punch line, they would all shout supersarcastically, "Ha ha ha ha ha," and then mega-straight-faced, "Hilarious." I bombed.

After graduating I happened to get a summer job at La Cantina—as a cocktail waitress. No one recognized me at first; it took Sheryl, the other waitress, about a week before she blurted, "Oh my god, you're that girl who tried to do comedy here that time." I stood helplessly as the rest of the staff gathered around, looking me over, making the connection. "Don't quit your day job," they laughed. Which was not only unoriginal but nonsensical, since I worked at night. With them. *There.* If memory serves me, Mozart had a nearly identical experience while working *his* summer job at a Salzburg alehouse.

I Finally Move to the City Where Practically Everyone Already Thought I Was From

Throughout my life, people have often assumed I'm from New York City. I imagine this is mostly due to my complete lack of a New Hampshire accent and my Jewiness. Even as a little girl, grown-ups would ask me, "Are you from New York?" This puzzled me—I'd never even been there.

"What's New York? I'm from here."

Maybe they knew something I didn't.

Manchester, New Hampshire, had a big theater called The Palace. It staged summer stock shows, where professional actors from New York came for the season, and put up three plays. As a teenager, I apprenticed at The Palace for two summers, painting the stage and performing whatever other menial tasks they handed me. But I also got to be part of the chorus, if the play of the moment had one, and to live in the cast-house dorm with the actors. I became good friends with many of them. In the winter, I went to New York to visit these friends whenever I could. Any time I had a gift coming to me—Hanukkah or my birthday—I would ask for a shuttle ticket from Boston to New York City (fifty bucks round-trip at the time). To this day, my mother looks back on that wondering what she was thinking, letting a fifteen-year-old girl go to New York City for the weekend, but I love that she did. These trips sparked an intense desire in me—to get out of New Hampshire and live in New York City on my own. The kid who was always afraid to sleep over at friends' houses traveled alone to New York feeling confident and adventurous. I flew and took the subway by myself. On my own in this incomprehensibly massive metropolis, I managed to navigate and stay alive. Even more than home, it felt like home.

To the lifelong aspiring performer part of me, New York was like a playground stocked with my favorite toys. I got to see *Les Misérables* on New Year's Eve 1986, because one of my friends from the summer worked the concession booth selling T-shirts. I desperately loved the soundtrack and dreamed of playing Eponine. Well before the curtain went up, my friend let me walk on the stage and I cried.

Seeing the play that night for the first time—until then I'd only listened to the soundtrack—I understood it in a whole new way. After the show I boarded the subway, looked down at my red Swatch, and watched it turn to midnight. I looked up at this train car full of strangers, and my heart soared. In New Hampshire, I'd always felt like a goat living among sheep; until I got to New York it had never occurred to me that there could be a place filled with other goats. It was the best New Year's I'd had yet. It probably still is.

At seventeen I took a train from New Hampshire to New York City to go to an open call for Gypsy.

In the fall of 1989 my mom came with me to New York City to help move me into my freshman dorm at NYU. We arrived in the city the night before and stayed at the Washington Square Hotel, putting the bulk of my luggage in their storage room. The next morning, we were given the storage key and went to gather my things. We opened the door, and there, lying on top of a mountain of luggage—including my trunk—was a maintenance man with his pants down around his ankles. His eyes locked with ours; he was in what I now understand to be the final unstoppable bucking stages of jerking off. A few very long seconds later he scrambled to get his pants up enough to scurry past us and out the door. At which point we piled my belongings into a big rolling cart and headed off to the dorm. To some, this might have seemed an ominous beginning to a new phase of life, but I found it oddly affirming. I guess at some level I viewed it as just one more sign of New York's immense diversity. I had spent my life feeling like the weird one in my community, *I* had been the masturbating maintenance man, if you will, of southern New Hampshire—but if there were people like this in New York, surely I could find a place for myself well inside the fringe.

Mom and I arrived at my room in Rubin Hall, at 5th Avenue and 10th Street, to find a boy in boxer shorts and a T-shirt sitting Indian-style with his back against my dorm room door, organizing a tray of cassette tapes. He introduced himself as Jason Steinberg, a sophomore, and gestured across the hall to his room. I could see through the open door that his walls were covered in Billy Joel posters. He was Jewish but looked Italian to me, straight out of *Saturday Night Fever*. I had never seen a Star of David worn like a cross around someone's neck.

He seemed to be a real mover and shaker. When he heard Mom and me discussing my need for a stereo of some kind, he took us to Crazy Eddie's and negotiated the lowest price for a tape player–radio. Lots of nights I would see him come home with full-grown women—the kind who wore fur coats. When I told him I was going to be a comedian, he mentioned that he worked the door at a place on West 3rd Street called Boston Comedy Club, got me a job passing out flyers there, and encouraged me to do their open mikes. I was sad the day he got kicked out of the dorm for calling my roommate a cunt.

The Corner

I passed out flyers for Boston Comedy Club on most days from 4:00 p.m. to 2:00 a.m. It was great money—ten bucks an hour. I was stationed at the corner of West 3rd and MacDougal, immersed in a culture of all ages, races, socioeconomic classes, and states of mental stability and sobriety.

I quickly became friends with all the corner drug dealers. Two in particular, named "English" and "Shady." Shady had big bulging eyes and wore a red bandana; English was black and British, and sported a full beard and mustache. He was tickled to be sharing his corner with this white, Jewish, wide-eyed girl, and took me under his wing, showing me where he'd buried knives—just in case I needed one. He hid them in various patches of garden and other public places where attempts had been made to bring nature into the city. I couldn't imagine a situation in which I would need a knife, let alone have time to dig one up, which in hindsight shows a lack of imagination, the kind that would have prevented me from enjoying a successful career in retail narcotics.

*   *   *

My post on the corner led to my first real friendship with a homeless guy (if you're a comic, sooner or later you will either befriend, financially support, or become a homeless person). His name was James, and he would walk me home at night through Washington Square Park. On one of these nights he said, "You know who you look like?" I assumed he was going to say Barbara Eden. Seriously, I used to get Barbara Eden a lot because I wore my hair in that *I Dream of Jeannie* kind of deal. Instead, he said, "Ken Wahl. From *Wiseguy*." I was half insulted, half bewildered—where the fuck was this guy watching TV? He sleeps outside of a restaurant in a deconstructed cardboard box.

James and I ride the subway.

James treated me like a princess. One time my parents' friends Arnie and Alice Goldstein came to see me perform at Boston Comedy Club, and as they approached the place, James was vigorously sweeping the sidewalk. Arnie said to him, tickled, "Look at this, very nice," to which James replied,

"I'm making it perfect for my Sarah!"

I had me a nice little family going there on that corner.

✻   ✻   ✻

There was another comic named Franz Cassius who also passed out flyers for the club. His were green and mine were orange. This system enabled Barry, the club owner, to calculate our weekly bonuses by determining exactly how many customers each of us was bringing in. Barry had bailed Franz out of Rikers Island and given him this job as well as letting him do occasional stand-up spots at the club. It was a while before I realized that Franz was just fucking around all night until right before each show when he'd infiltrate the line and trade the patrons my flyers for his, explaining, "These flyers are better."

*   *   *

Over the weeks and months of working that corner I began to understand English's impulse to bury knives. I was just dealing flyers, not Schedule I narcotics, and still found a fair amount of trouble. One night I noticed a dead-eyed homeless Vietnam vet in full battle fatigues marching straight toward me. I did the only thing I could think of: I extended a flyer to him and chirped, "Free comedy?" Without a word or break in stride, he leaped at me and wrapped his hands around my throat. Passersby pulled him off me almost instantly—what is that Tennessee Williams line about depending on the kindness of strangers?—and though I was shaken, not ten minutes later I was back to my barking duties.

I shared the corner with another flyer-hander-outer—the mascot from Pluck-U Chicken, a nearby fast-food establishment. You might scoff that puns don't whet the appetite, but that place was insanely popular with NYU students. The mascot was an Asian kid my age in a giant chicken suit. To do that job shows tremendous ambition. Not because it leads anywhere, but because it means he was faced with the questions: What is it worth to you to go to college? What are you willing to do to afford the best education possible? Would you put on a chicken suit and stand on the meanest corner the weekend has ever seen? His answer was, Yes. Yes, he would.

Weekends were the worst time to be on the corner because it was packed with Bridge and Tunnelers—in this case, mostly seventeen-year-old guys from Jersey who were drunk and scarier than any junkie crook or deranged vet.

One unfortunate Saturday, a group of these boys took interest in the Chicken. They started throwing beer from their 40-ouncers onto his feathers as the Chicken tried to defend himself with meek, sotto-voced *"Don't"*'s. One of the guys started pushing him. He was a tall, skinny, blond douche bully. I got between them and said to the guy, "Hey, hands off." Note that this was not bravery or heroism, it was just me really overestimating my cuteness; in a million years it didn't occur to me that I could possibly be harmed. But the next thing I knew, I was knocked off my feet with a blow square to the temple.

I came to, encircled by strangers. My head hurt, I was freaked out, and I just burst into tears like a baby. Franz Cassius ran over, demanding a description of the guy who punched me. He was to-tally jazzed at having a good excuse to beat the shit out of a white boy. "White, thin, tall, blond, carrying a forty-ounce," I told him, and Franz took off without so much as a "How are you?" or a "Can I help you off the ground?" If I were a betting man, I'd say there was probably more than one white, thin, tall guy who met Franz's fist that night.

Forced to Choose Between Earning a Bachelor's Degree and Handing Out Pieces of Orange Paper to Strangers, I Do the Sensible Thing

Up to this point, I'd always been a good student. But because I was working from 4:00 p.m. till 2:00 a.m., I was finding it almost impossible to keep my eyes open in class. I was a drama major, so most of my courses were fairly easy to negotiate even in a state of unconsciousness, but not all of them. With those that required any semblance of sentience, I was having trouble. Still, giving up my sweet gig on the corner wasn't an option. Had it occurred to me that for the price of two years of my education at NYU, I could have *bought* Boston Comedy Club, I might have succumbed to futility and quit. But that's the whole trick when you're starting out as a stand-up comic—not to succumb to futility.

Anyway, it wasn't entirely futile. I began to make progress. I passed an important comic's milestone: I got to go onstage without having to barter two paying customers for the privilege. I did open mikes all over the city and soon reached another milestone: I "passed" at the Comic Strip. Meaning that after the owner, Lucian, saw my open-mike performance, he said I could call in regularly to leave my availability for the week and wait to hear if I landed any spots. The comics were paid ten dollars a set on weeknights, fifty dollars on weekends. I worked as much as I could. If I didn't have a spot, I would just hang out and try to get on.

My niece came out of the closet yesterday. She's seven. My sister said she's ~~gonna~~ gonna punish her. Ain't that awful? No pussy for a week.

In that era, the comics who got all the stage time included Mark Cohen, Dave Attell, Ray Romano, Kevin Brennan, Louis C.K., Chris Rock, Susie Essman, Jay Mohr, and Jon Stewart, among others. Jay would skateboard from set to set. Jon hadn't been at it long, but he was great right away. Mike Sweeney, who became the head writer at Conan O'Brien's show, was also amazing. I was so in love with him. He mostly worked around the corner at the Comedy Cellar as the emcee back when emcees were the stars of the show. Mike rarely bothered with prepared material. He just talked to the audience and was hilarious. Mike Royce, who went on to write and produce *Everybody Loves Raymond*, was another regular. After finishing their sets at the Comedy Cellar, Royce and Romano would sit in a booth at the restaurant upstairs going over their jokes and sets. They were so studious. Jeff Lifschultz, now Jeff Ross—Comedy Central's reigning "Roast Master"—and Todd Barry, soft-spoken and brutally hilarious, started out around the same time as me, so we spent many nights together in the backs of clubs, hoping a scheduled comic would cancel and one of us would get on.

After freshman year, I decided to take the next year off. I wanted to pursue stand-up more seriously. I also wanted to remember what it was like to sleep in a bed rather than in the back of a classroom at the cost of, let's say, thirty dollars a minute. It was a solid year of writing jokes, having sex, and doing all sorts of psychedelic drugs.

One night, after hanging out at the Comedy Cellar and trying to get on stage, we went upstairs to The Olive Tree, a restaurant where all the comics hung out after their sets. It was 1:30 in the morning and I was sitting with my buddy Dave Juskow, whom I had met through my then-boyfriend Dave Attell. An old hippie guy came in and handed us two tabs of acid. I honestly don't remember how this happened, but without a thought, we popped it in our mouths. For the next thirteen and a half hours, Dave and I went bananas. We wound up hanging out with semihomeless strangers in Washington Square Park, experiencing every possible emotion. It happened to be the third of July and already firecrackers were going off everywhere; we were convinced we were at war. About five hours into it we decided we didn't want to be tripping anymore, we wanted to go through the motions of normal life. Not that this was up to us.

We walked to Dave's car, got in, and pulled out to the street. As we sat at a red light, Dave realized he had forgotten how to drive. The light turned green and we both panicked, paralyzed as it turned to yellow, red, and back to green again. Luckily, it was early in the morning and we were on a side street, so there were no cars yet behind us. I switched seats with Dave, but as it turned out, I didn't remember how to drive, either. We were sure that a cop was going to pull up beside us any minute. I popped out of the car, went to a phone booth, and dialed the one number I could remember—Louie C.K.'s. Louie was usually up all night and into the morning—not experimenting with drugs so much as teaching himself Russian or how to play guitar. He picked up the phone and calmly talked me through.

"You know how to drive. Don't think about it, just let your body remember. You are fine and you can do this."

I got back into the car and, as mindlessly as I could, parked it. Dave and I decided that Louie was God as we walked back to my apartment, the city now beginning to hum with early morning commuter traffic. We made it to my little room and played my roommate's Squeeze *Singles* album over and over. Then, fully clothed, we went into the shower and turned on the water. In movies, people trying to get sober were always taking cold showers in their clothes, so it seemed like the right thing to do.

My year off was filled with a lot of these nights. Not all of them involved LSD trips, per se, but they were all, as the '70s would say, "pretty far out." I won't go so far as to say that these experiences are necessary rites of passage on the way to a well-rounded adulthood, but I figured they had to be more enriching than snoozing in the back of a classroom.

*   *   *

When it was time to register for my sophomore year, I decided to change my major from drama to arts and sciences. My dream was still to be a comedian and an actor, and in pursuit of that, I decided I would have more to glean from academic classes than the voice and movement-type classes that made up the bulk of the drama curriculum.

Two weeks before the fall term started, Dad called and made me a proposition. He said, "I wouldn't do this with any of my other girls but I feel like you know what you want to do, and it doesn't take a college degree. I believe in you, and if you wanna drop out of school, I'll pay for your rent and utilities for what would have been your sophomore, junior, and senior years. That way I save twenty grand a year and you get to pursue your dream full time."

Needless to say, I'm very glad he did this, but sometimes, in quiet moments, I wonder: At what cost to the world? If I'd stayed in college, and been really inspired by, say, a biology class, I might have become a world-renowned entomologist. Right now I could be saving the Rocky Mountains from pine beetle devastation. But instead: fart jokes and blasphemy. Smooth move, Dad.

*   *   *

My roommate Beth Tapper naked and in front of our refrigerator

For most of my time in New York, I lived at 129 Second Avenue between 7th Street and St. Marks Place on the fifth floor of a six-floor walk-up. My roommate Beth and I were lucky—we had our own toilet, whereas many of the apartments shared a padlocked bathroom in the hallway. One resident on our floor had recently gotten out of prison, which I knew because the day he moved in, he looked at me and said, "I just got out of prison!" with the joy one would say, "I'm going to Disneyworld!" and the crazy eyes with which someone might say, "I just stabbed a hooker in the face!"

I didn't see him much, mostly because I made a point of waiting to leave my apartment until any sign of life in the hallway vanished.

One night, as Beth and I were heading down the long winding stairwell, he and a friend were walking behind us. We didn't think much of it until he dropped what was evidently an enormous box of bullets. The steel cartridges poured down the stairs and through our legs down to the landing, making a loud, rhythmic *tap tap tap*, like the closing number from *STOMP* (which coincidentally was playing across the street at the Orpheum Theater). Beth and I kept walking like nothing was happening. As if there were no bullets smacking our heels or tripping up our steps.

Honoring the Deal with My Father, I Get Serious—but Also High and Naked

College seems to be as much about making friends and connections as it is about actual learning. I've heard that at Oxford there's very little structured academic life; it's mostly just people drinking beer at pubs, engaging in all manner of intellectual exchange. If that's true, then this was my Oxford period. Except that instead of being brainy Rhodes scholars passionate about knowledge and destined to lead the world, we were comics passionate about dick jokes and destined for a spot on *Premium Blend*. But like our counterparts at Oxford, our lives were consumed with experimentation and exploration.

One of my best friends during that time was Louie C.K., then and now a brilliant and prolific comic. Louie lived in a building on Bleecker Street called the Atrium—and it was one. The apartments looked down onto the first-floor lobby. He owned almost nothing. His belongings consisted of a bed, a record player, and a computer. He used the walls for making notes; they were covered with scribbled reminders to himself, various lists, and people's phone numbers.

At about 2:00 a.m. one night we started daring each other to throw our clothes over the balcony down into the atrium. I don't remember who tossed the first article, but from there we took turns removing a single piece of clothing, dropping it into the void, and watching it float down to the lobby, sometimes catching on the branches of indoor hedges. Each round became more and more daring since we were less and less covered, until we were both naked. Totally naked. And just when you think you can't get more daring than that, we climbed into the elevator and rode it down to the lobby, giggling with terror at the possibility that the elevator could stop at any floor, or that once we got to the bottom any number of residents could be walking in. The doors opened at lobby level, and we scrambled to gather our clothes and manically get dressed. We rode the elevator back up to Louie's floor, and as we approached the safety of his apartment, a shirt flew past his head and over the balcony. He turned to see me, shirtless again, wearing just a bra.

We wound up doing eleven full cycles of this. We laughed harder each time because, in addition to the obvious risk of getting caught, there was the absurdity of the fact that we were doing the same fucking thing—chasing the same high—over and over again. This must be why people bungee jump.

The stunt was emblematic of our lives during that period. When all of your friends are comedians and you spend your life in a club hearing and telling jokes, it becomes ever more challenging to make each other laugh. I imagine it's like working in porn—after a while, missionary just doesn't cut it anymore. You need a midget and a monkey and a bottle of Head & Shoulders to get any kind of boner.

Once, Louie and I were standing on the corner just outside my apartment, making each other laugh. I had just woken up and thrown on a skirt and T-shirt to meet him for breakfast at the Waverly Diner downstairs. I said, "Louie, look down." He looked and I peed straight onto the sidewalk. Just a tiny bit. One single staccato, creating the onomatopoeia *Bloop*.

I was pretty convinced I was adorable.

*   *   *

Beth and I lived two floors above Todd Barry, who would frequently show up at our door, not quite to borrow a cup of sugar, but instead for the neighborly request of, say, shaving the back of his neck. Todd is a hilarious comic with no real quirks in his onstage persona, but offstage is famous for his random verbal tics. For years, the word "AIDS" popped out of his mouth in a nonsensical, quasi-Tourettes-like manner. "What's up? AIDS." Over time "AIDS" was replaced with "Apologize."

"Wanna get coffee?"

"Sure."

"Apologize."

Todd had a long-standing fake feud with Louie C.K., which manifested in verbal-tic phrases such as, "Louie's not funny." "Louie's the mayor of unfunnytown," and a chant he orchestrated with Beth and me:

> TODD: *I fucked Louie's mom.*
>
> US: *You didn't. You didn't.*
>
> TODD: *I fucked Louie's mom.*
>
> US: *You didn't. You didn't.*

TODD: *I fucked Louie's mom.*

US: *You didn't. You didn't. You didn't fuck Louie's mom.*

TODD: *Louie's not funny. He's bad at what he does. He's bad at stand-up comedy and everything he loves.*

No one loves this song more than Louie.

*Todd Barry and I ride the subway to our show
at Carnegie Hall, November 7, 2007.*

Life at that time was all about who would push it the farthest, who could be the most uncivilized just for a laugh. Brian Posehn was a comic who moved to L.A. from San Francisco, armed with a soon-to-be-classic bit in his arsenal—not a stage bit but one just for comics. He called it "Accidental Blowjob Guy." It went like this: If you're laughing at something another comic said, you turn the laugh into a sudden, gagging faux blowjob of that comic. That one spread like wildfire among us. At a wrap party for the second season of HBO's *Mr. Show*, while Brian and Mark Cohen were standing around cracking each other up, they both simultaneously went in for the blowjob and smashed heads, resulting in something ten times funnier than the bit itself. Mark broke his nose on the back of Brian's head. HE BROKE HIS NOSE GIVING A FAKE BLOW-JOB. Holy shit. I love that story with every part of me.

By now, just as the Oxford crowd has left the pub to take up their stations in the highest echelons of world power, my comic friends and I have grown up. Only *not*.

MAKE IT A TREAT

My Guide to Drugs, Alcohol, Sex, and Other Things That Have the Potential to Be Gross

First, I'll take advantage of this mass media format to address a small matter that needs clarification: Those who know of me know that I love doody jokes, but that is very different than loving *doody*. I make rape jokes, but I certainly don't approve of rape. These nuances might seem obvious to you, but there are people out there who think they are fans of mine, feel we are kindred spirits, and want very much to show me pictures of their poop and other extremely disgusting things. And it gets worse.

One night I was at the Hollywood Improv and a famous musician from the '80s approached me with a few of his friends. I was a big fan and very excited to meet him. He said, "You are my favorite comedian! I loved *Jesus Is Magic!*" I was so excited, I gushed,

"Thank you so much, I'm a big fan of yours—"

"You have the best nigger jokes!"

"Well, I don't . . . that's not how I—"

"She's got the best nigger jokes!" he repeated to his friends.

It was pretty horrifying. It probably can best be described as what an old boyfriend would call a "mouth full of blood laughs," when a person in the audience is laughing at the wrong thing—the ugly part of the joke—the part intended for irony or insidiousness. It would be uncouth to divulge this musician's identity, though the wide-eyed earnestness with which he employed the word "nigger" leads me to believe he sees no fault in his use of it, as he sees no fault (or difference) in the way I had used it. But I will tell you that after that incident I *Stopped Believin'*.

I know that all this crap is what I should expect when I choose to build a career on shock and profanity, but since I've got this book, I'm going to try to get the message out: I'm not interested in seeing pictures of anyone's bowel movements. The two exceptions would be (1) Clive Owen's, for obvious reasons; and (2) Nelson Mandela's, because his life has just been such an incredibly rich journey.

This all relates to the larger point of this chapter: That I am not an animal. Of course I am *literally* an animal, but I mean "I am not an animal" the way the Elephant Man meant it (though he was pretty gross). I feel I have life pretty much figured out, and I would now like to share this gift with you. I have a mantra, and that is: "Make It a Treat." Look, there's not much useful to take away from this book—it's largely stories of a woman who has spent her life peeing on herself. But there is one way I really believe I can help the world, and that is to encourage everyone, in all things, to "Make It a Treat."

This maxim was introduced to me by my friend Kerry (you know, the descendant of African royalty from a few brilliant chapters ago). It happened when we were freshmen in college. She came up from Howard University to visit me at NYU and found me smoking pot like a disgusting fiend all day. I offered her a hit of my joint and she waved me off. I didn't understand. I knew she smoked pot. "Just because I take a puff sometimes doesn't mean I'm gonna make a career of it, " Kerry explained. " If you want to enjoy these things—things like weed—you have to make it a treat."

I've had very few epiphanies while being extremely stoned that have endured. Mostly they evaporate like mist at the moment I start munching pizza. (An exception that comes to mind is "2-3-1-7-8." I found it to be an extremely hilarious sequence of numbers when I was stoned, and as you can see in sobriety's harsh glare, it remains so.) But Kerry's tiny pearl of wisdom struck me, and stuck with me. For a four-word, off-the-cuff dictum, it has had a surprisingly large impact on my life.

"Make It a Treat" is similar in spirit to "everything in moderation," but still very distinct. "Moderation" suggests a regular, low-level intake of something. MIAT asks for more austerity; it encourages you to keep the special things in life *special*. I apply this rule in a variety of ways. For instance, I wear makeup and high heels on special occasions. But if I dressed up all the time, it would become ordinary, and I would receive fewer compliments. If makeup and heels was my everyday look, I would be met with disappointed reactions if, one day, I went out in a hoodie and sneakers. Instead, it's the opposite: A hoodie and sneakers are my everyday look, so on those rare occasions when I do dress up, or put any effort into my appearance at all, it's met with "Look at you!"

Nowhere do I find myself invoking MIAT more than in the writers' room of my television show. My writing staff is a bubbling cauldron of primordial id (more on this in another chapter), and I'm not far ahead of them on the evolution chart. There is a constant clamor to introduce farts, both into the scripts and our immediate atmosphere. I have—not just for a female, but any human being—an inordinate love of farts (jokes involving them, that is; though I don't personally emit them—*ever*). Fart jokes make me happier than just about anything in the universe. And for that reason I'm terrified by the idea that someday I might have had enough of them. If they are a genuine treat and a surprise, they are the surest way to send me into tear-soaked convulsions of laughter. (For any devoted fans of the show who happen to be reading this, I realize that in a particular episode of season two, there were roughly thirty-seven farts, but in that instance they were essential to the plot and emotional stakes, so we had no choice but to make an exception.)

Another treat in my show's comedy cookie jar is Steve Agee's gagging and dry heaving. If you're not familiar with it, a written description won't help. It's just hilarious. No other element of the show has forced me to *shout*, "MAKE IT A TREAT!!" like Steve's gagging has. To yank "STEVE GAGS" out of a script is easy. But I can't be on the set for every scene. So I'll be sitting in the editing room watching a cut, and goddamnit, there that motherfucker is, doing an unscripted dry heave. Sometimes he'll do a very subtle one, like he thinks if I'm not watching carefully, he can slip it past me. But since I watch each episode literally dozens of times before they're finalized, I'll eventually catch it and, ignoring the editor's pleading expression, I order it cut. I do this because I *love* to watch Steve gag, and I never want to stop loving it. Being a standard-bearer can be lonely, but I know I'm doing it for the greater good. You're welcome on that.

And then, of course, there is pot. Since that moment with Kerry, I treat pot with the sacredness it deserves. I smoke it the way one might have a glass of wine with dinner. On certain days of the week, when my work is done, and I am sure that I have no intellectual responsibilities left, I take *one puff*, maybe two, and relax. On special occasions, I literally make it a treat, and eat a pot brownie.

I'll be honest; I have contempt for pretty much every drug other than pot. I find drunk people gross. Most people with more than one drink in them aren't giggly, goofy, and happy the way people are with a puff of pot smoke in them. In the best case, a drunk person rambles, shares way too much uncomfortable information, and embarrasses himself instead of amusing others. Just as often, drunks are sullen, hostile, wobbly, slurry, and smelly. They talk way too close to my face, and their self-consciousness level rises to such a degree that if you blink at them wrong, they wanna know what your problem is. At a party, I have so much fun stoned, flitting about—but once I sniff that first wave of drunkenness on someone, I'm out of there. To me, it's a signal that tells me it's time to head to a diner and finish the night right. With eggs.

I find that people are generally less able to make alcohol a treat than pot. Alcohol tends to be a regular habit, and lots of drinkers don't cut themselves off after a reasonable amount—they just keep drinking until there is none left.

Whoever designed cocaine intended it as an attack on "Make It a Treat." The only thing that snorting a line of coke leads to is snorting more lines of coke. Coke turns people into coke fiends. That fact wouldn't bother me necessarily, if they could ever just shut the fuck up. But that is exactly what coked-up people *cannot do.* And with the possible exception of Richard Pryor, cocaine leads to not-shutting-up about profoundly boring things. I was recently at a party, and got ear-raped by a guy too wired to see that I had no interest in his passionate lecture about Egyptian furniture. Coke and booze, to me, are just not chemically designed for self-control; they don't facilitate the mind-set of making things sacred. Coke makes everyone, without exception, huge douchebags.

I turn now to sex, and the Internet video watching thereof. I think it's imperative that for the good of society, we should all strive to make porn a treat. That has been especially challenging for me as I write this book because, of course, I am at home, at my desk, on my laptop, at all times one click away from watching people fuck—and in the most fascinating, shocking ways. The reasons for making porn a treat are fairly obvious: Like any image you spend lots of time looking at, it shapes your brain. If I'm watching porn every day, I'm allowing my brain to be shaped by *the people who work in porn.* I may masturbate to them, but I certainly don't revere them. I'm compelled to point out that porn actors, more than anyone else on the planet, have no sense of "Make It a Treat." They spend their lives making unspecial the most special thing in the world. I wish they made porn starring people whom I do actually respect. It might be cool to have watched Eunice Kennedy, who started the Special Olympics, have sex with one of those Doctors Without Borders guys—they're so amazing.

I've been very prescriptive, and at moments just flat-out judgmental in this chapter, and it's about to get a little worse. I am going to recommend that you also make anal sex a treat. In my own life, it's nonexistent. I am one of those people who believe that anuses are filthy (except mine; you could eat off mine—it's been scientifically proven). Again, doody comes out of tushies—mine excepted—and that's gross.

(Time out for a second, and please note that I largely direct this advice to heterosexuals, as the issues for gay men are logistically different. Aaaaand time in.)

Regardless of nature's plans for my asshole, a large foreign object up there is, well, what's a stronger phrase meaning "not my cup of tea"? I understand and respect that you might be different. So, if you must, may I at least suggest that you apply ample lubrication and a generous dollop of MIAT? Presumably, at the deepest level, you enjoy anal sex because it's forbidden and dangerous and perverse. That allure and mystery will be more successfully preserved if you keep the lube in the attic instead of the bedside drawer.

I am a creature of habit, so to make anything that I really love a treat is often a challenge. One colleague cleverly told me that my insistence on making things a treat should, itself, be made a treat. I recall saying "touché" but also thinking that I wouldn't mind firing him. Actually, that's often how I feel when I'm saying "touché" to someone. I don't follow my own or anyone else's advice all the time. But that's why mantras need to be repeated—they're fucking hard to remember. So a heartfelt thanks to Kerry—the friend I deeply adore but get to enjoy only on special occasions.

LIVE FROM NEW YORK, YOU'RE FIRED

The Happiest I Have Ever Been in a Public Toilet

In 1993, when I was twenty-two, I flew to Los Angeles to meet with Jim Downey and Lorne Michaels (the executive producer and head writer nonrespectively, of *Saturday Night Live*). They were looking to hire new writer-performers for the upcoming season, and I was one candidate among many to be interviewed. To the meeting, I wore my hair mostly down, with two small ponytails pulled off my face, mimicking a picture of Gilda Radner that had always stuck in my mind. Later that night, I was invited to the *Coneheads* premiere at Grauman's Chinese Theatre, and that's where my manager informed me that I'd gotten the job.

If women could ejaculate, I would have exploded hot jizz all over my manager's face. Instead, I hugged him. The only thing that kept me from melting to the floor was the fact that I was bouncing up to the ceiling. I could not believe it. I wanted to tell *everyone*. Nothing in the world—at least for a comedian—could be better than telling your friends that you're going to be on *Saturday Night Live*. Telling those very people with whom you reenacted all the "Sweeney Sisters" musical numbers, telling your mother who never said "cheeseburger" or "Pepsi" the same way after 1975. I don't know what to compare it to. I guess if you fixed clocks for a living, it'd be like getting to fix Big Ben.

Learning you've been hired and telling everyone you know is one of the great joys of the *SNL* experience. And here it was happening to me. In the middle of a movie theater in L.A. where I didn't know anyone and at a time when only assholes owned cellphones. So I did the only thing I could do: I went to the bathroom, locked myself in a stall, and just . . . beamed.

I Am Awakened to the Existence of Harvard, and to My Not Having Gone There

The basic *SNL* workweek went like this: Monday, we would go to Lorne's office, meet the guest host, and take turns pitching our sketch ideas; the host would smile and nod and pretend to like all of them. Then we'd go off and start writing. You worked on the sketches you pitched, although if any other writers took an interest they might offer to collaborate and vice versa. On Tuesday, it was tradition to write all night long, all the way through to Wednesday's table read at 4:00 p.m.

My office was adjacent to another writer, named Ian Maxtone Graham. He was everything his three-name name suggests. Someone told me he never got his license because he grew up always having drivers.

Knowing that Ian Maxtone Graham grew up with drivers, it might shock you to learn that he wasn't the most hoity-toity of the writers there. The *Harvard Lampoon* has always been a breeding ground for *SNL* writers, and these guys were practically born with ascots. To give you an idea, they regularly teased *Ian Maxtone Graham* (you really have to say the whole name) for only having gone to *Brown*. It had never occurred to me before that there was such a strong connection between elite schools and funniness, although, to be honest, it still doesn't occur to me. That's a generalization, though. Some Harvard grads have been true comedy legends, like Al Franken, Conan O'Brien, and George Meyer.

The year I was at *SNL* the staff was a crazy combination of *Harvard Lampoon*ers (the old ones who had been there since the beginning, and the new ones who had graduated that May and had little to qualify them other than that) and stand-up comedians (myself, Dave Attell, Jay Mohr, and Norm MacDonald). There was a palpable class division.

There was also an age gap. Four of us were only twenty-two years old—me and the three most recent Harvard graduates. On our first day of work, we were introduced to each other and sent off to the NBC commissary for lunch. We talked and laughed all through lunch until one of the guys said to me, "So what do you do in the office? Type?"

Lacking Adult Coping Skills, I Steal Clean Underwear

By around 2:00 a.m. Wednesday mornings, I'd start to feel gamey and uncomfortable from being in the same clothes for so long. I'm not sure how I justified this in my head, but I would slip into Ian Maxton Graham's office, where he had one drawer of fresh boxers and one drawer of fresh socks, and, without his permission or knowledge, I would take one of each and put them on. Inevitably we'd cross paths during the night, and he'd discover me wearing his giant boxer shorts (which came down to my knees) and freshly laundered tube socks (which came up to my knees). I looked at him like, "Go ahead and say something." But he never did. I suppose my raids on Ian Maxtone Graham's underwear were not just an attempt to get comfortable and feel fresh, but also a sort of subconscious waging of micro—class warfare. All of this is really too much to expect from underwear, even if it belongs to someone named Ian Maxtone Graham.

1994: Tuesday all-nighter at SNL. Crouched on a tabletop writing a soon-to-never-be-seen-on-TV sketch. Note my freshly stolen boxers and socks, courtesy of one unwitting Ian Maxtone Graham.

By Some Fluke, My Genius Is Overlooked, Twenty-five Weeks in a Row

On Wednesdays at 4:00 p.m., the cast, crew, and host sat at an enormous table and read each script aloud. Afterward, the host would hole up in Lorne's office, and the two of them would decide which sketches would be produced. By around 8:00 p.m., Lorne opened his office door and the writers poured in to see if their sketches were on the 5-x-7 cards pinned up on his bulletin board.

One morning, Phil Hartman put his arm around me and said I should write something for us to do together. This moment of paternal encouragement randomly collided in my brain with an odd bit of trivia I'd recently picked up: That flies live for only twenty-four hours. I wrote a sketch in which Phil and I were father-daughter flies on a wall. By the end, he's on his deathbed. It cut to a dog taking a shit. Phil's last words were: "Go get it. It's beautiful." But neither this nor any other sketch I wrote ever made it past dress rehearsal.

☆   ☆   ☆

Thursdays were rewrite days. We would work on and off from noon to about 6:00 a.m. Friday, tweaking and punching up the sketches for that week's show. One thing I learned over the years since then is that the hours you work on a show are directly related to the happiness of the head writer's marriage. Jim Downey was in the marriage-not-so-good category, so we never really left work. Ever. This guy *did not want to go home*. Jim was another Harvard grad. He'd been at *SNL* since the beginning, and everyone, including me, worshipped him.

On Thursdays we would all sit around a gigantic table, each of us with our own copies of that week's chosen scripts. In the center of the table were piles of legal pads and cups filled with the sharpest, most perfect pencils.

The cast and crew rehearsed Thursday and Friday, with script changes coming to them throughout. Saturday, of course, was show day. The writers would come in late morning and write jokes with Kevin Nealon for "Weekend Update." (Kevin is the kindest and funniest man you will ever meet.)

*   *   *

John Malkovich hosted one of the first episodes of the season. I got my first sketch on that week—one that I wrote for him and Mike Myers. I was so excited, I called my whole family to tell them to watch. The sketch took place backstage in the *SNL* hallway. Mike is at the water fountain, and John comes over and makes Mike do all his famous characters for him. It's awkward, but Mike does it because he's such a huge fan of John's. Then Jay Mohr comes over and asks John for an autograph, and John is an asshole to him. You get the picture.

After seeing my work performed at dress rehearsal, I was so giddy, I was on the brink of exploding, or at the very least skipping. It was my first piece to be actually performed in front of a live audience. After getting hired and telling people you have the job, that's the next genuine thrill to be had at *SNL*. With the exception of the Saturday-morning omelet station.

As was standard, after dress rehearsal we poured into Lorne's office for notes. I sat on the floor and pretended to listen, but really just daydreamed about the storm of postshow accolades I'd be happily braving in just two short hours. John Malkovich, sitting in a chair next to me, leaned down to say, "I'm so sorry I fucked up that one line!"

Aw! How sweet is that? Adorable. I reassured him, "Oh my god, don't worry about it, you were great! It's going to be GREAT!"

I couldn't stop smiling. Then Mike Myers turned to me and snapped,

"The sketch is *cut*, Sarah—look—the card is on the left side of the line," referring to the 5-x-7 card representing my sketch, and how it was on the "nope" half of Lorne's bulletin board.

That wiped the smile off my face good. I had to use all my strength not to crash through the floor.

Maybe it's obvious to most people that a ninety-minute weekly comedy show for live television on a major network is not—and cannot be—an especially nurturing environment. But somehow, that came as a surprise to me. I'm not sure what I expected. Maybe because *SNL* is an old, grand institution, I thought it would be like college, where they show you around, give you a formal orientation, and alert you to all the resources available for guidance and support. But at *SNL*, nobody puts a hand on your shoulder and says, "This was a good effort, it's just missing X or Y." There's no time for that. Still, I was all of twenty-two, and I'd been fully toilet trained for only six years. I really could have used a little mentoring. I bet even the Harvard boys could have, too.

Not Fearing Cliché, I Fall in Love with a Man Twice My Age During a Vulnerable Period in My Life

I was painfully in love with the head writer, Jim Downey. He told the best stories and was very calm and soft-spoken. If you made Jim Downey laugh, it was the biggest score. And, of course, he was an amazing—the best—writer.

One night, I handed in a script for Martin Lawrence, who was hosting that week. I gave it directly to Jim to read and waited on the couch outside his office for him to finish talking to John Bowman (the creator and executive producer of Martin's sitcom). Waiting on the couch turned into sleeping on the couch until 6:00 in the morning, when he and John finally walked out of his office. I popped up and asked, "Did you read it?"

"Read what?"

Jim had somehow lost the pages, and he laughed at my exhausted and frustrated tears. Still, I loved him.

Bittersweet News: It Takes Longer Than You'd Think to Make Me Look Like an Ape

At the beginning of December that year, Charlton Heston hosted, so of course the opening was a *Planet of the Apes* sketch. We actually got all the original costumes to use. I was going to play an ape in the audience, and, because I was a peon, I was put into all the prosthetics at noon on Saturday, so that the makeup people were not rushed for the important stuff later in the day. This sucked for obvious reasons—walking around with an ape face (more than my usual simian mug) for thirteen hours is uncomfortable to say the very least, but what made it so very much worse was that homegirl had the flu. My nose was running like crazy. Running, mind you, underneath a *fake face*. It was so uncomfortable that I actually started *weeping*. As it turns out, tears and snot do not mix well with glue and skin. My face was simultaneously cold, wet, and on fire, which I concede, in retrospect, is hilarious.

Dave Attell and me twelve hours into having faces glued onto our faces

I wore this used winter coat I got at Andy's Chee-Pee's, which had a fake fur collar, and someone took the greatest Polaroid of me bundled in it with my hood on and an ape's face sleeping in the fetal position on the couch in the writers' room.

Al Franken and Me:
A Friendship Is Born

I always sat next to Al Franken on rewrite Thursdays. I don't even know if he liked or had any interest in me personally or professionally, but some part of me decided he was *home base*. Maybe because he was a father, and for all intents and purposes, I was a kid. And he seemed nice under his tough exterior.

Al and Rob Schneider would have screaming fights—it was nuts—but often Al would come in the next day and say, "Hey, Rob, you know I thought about what I said to you yesterday and I'm really sorry." Or, "You know what? I think you were right after all." I found his self-reflection endearing. It was kind of lovely.

A couple months into my time there, Al came to me and apologized, though I could not imagine what for. He explained, "I thought your 'nice person' thing was an act, but then I saw you downstairs in the subway station and strangers asked you for directions, and I watched you show them where to go and you were so pleasant, and I know you couldn't see me, so I knew it was real."

"Oh. Thank you—er—I'm glad." I was grateful, but wow— what kind of world are you living in when you are so totally moved by common courtesy?

From then on, my usual spot in the writers' room was next to sweet Al Franken.

Al Franken and Me, Part Two: The Violent End

One day, a day like any other, I sat on the back legs of my chair, my feet hooked under the big writers' table. I was daydreaming, which I tended to do in between medium-sized stretches of focus.

I chewed the metal part of my pencil, the part that holds the eraser, pinching it down, then twisting it twenty-five degrees to bite down and right it back to its circular demeanor. As I noticed the über-sharpened tip of my pencil, my eyes wandered to Al's giant full-out Jew 'fro (they grow them big in the winter for warmth), and I thought to myself, "I'm gonna spear this pencil right through Al's big afro."

I don't think I thought that with actual words. It's weird now to try to articulate it that way. However the mind works when it's not forming sentences—with pictures maybe? I guess yes, perhaps maybe I pictured it—I envisioned myself playfully poking my pencil through his thick, curly, Jewy, wiry locks. Yes.

My body set itself in motion in a knee-jerk attempt to reenact what my brain had mapped out less than a second previously. I followed said map exactly. Unfortunately, due to what I realize now must have been a gross miscalculation of where his hair started and his head ended, what I meant to do and what everyone *saw with their eyeballs* were two very different things.

From thought to action, what happened was that, seemingly out of nowhere, I just turned and, *boom*, stabbed Al Franken square in the temple. He responded with a horrifying scream—his eyes wide in angry, mystified shock (like, say, a man who'd just been stabbed in the head by the person sitting next to him). I wanted so much to account for my actions but I couldn't. Besides it being a sort of challenging scenario to explain, I also *couldn't* explain, as I was literally breathless from laughing—like, hysterically laughing. I was a mad-woman crazy-person with tears pouring down my face. I can imagine how it must have looked. Even the explanation, had I had the breath to clarify, let's face it, was weirdo weird.

I'll never know for sure the exact reason, but that August my agent got a fax asking me not to return for a second season. I can't actually say which I'd rather believe—that I was fired for stabbing Al Franken in the head, or because in twenty-five weeks, I'd gotten exactly no sketches on the air. I guess I'd prefer the former, since, like any comedian, I'd rather have my sanity questioned than my skill.

In November of 2008, I saw Al at a pre-inaugural party in Washington, D.C. He was in the midst of recount torture after his senatorial election. I was so happy to see him—I ran over, "Al!" I could feel his whole body tense amid my big bear hug so I released him.

"Hello, Sarah," he said, equal parts polite, appropriate, cold, and . . . almost . . . frightened? You know when you totally over-estimate a friendship? Where a big hello hug meets a rigid rape-victimish stance? It was like that. I said, "Did you hear I talked about you on *Letterman*?" I had told the stabbing-Al-in-the-head story earlier that year.

He said, "Yes, I heard about it, though I can't say I remember that."

"You don't remember me stabbing you in the fucking HEAD??"

"Well, I hope I wasn't too angry with you." He said it like the Stepford wife I knew he wasn't.

I said, "No, not at all—only appropriately so."

I looked to his right and left and saw he was with a couple of big faceless men. We talked for a bit longer and he softened. He

Finally, Laura, the middle child, gets a picture taken just of her when this asshole (me) sneaks in like, "Look at me! I have a red ball!"

All four sisters, 1979: Jodyne, Susie, Laura, me, and our baby cousin, Abby.

This is a game I like to call "Find the Jew."

All four sisters, 1992: Me, Rabbi Susie, Jodyne, and Laura lying across us.

My NYC apartment, 1994. Mark Cohen plays guitar—notice the colored tampons decorating the wall in the background.

New York magazine did a story in 1995 on NY comics that featured Marc Maron, Louis C.K., Dave Attell, and me. They put us in these fancy outfits, which may or may not be the reason we all look miserable.

My roommates for the first three years of living in L.A.: Mary Lynn Rajskub (now Chloe O'Brian on *24*) and Tracy Katsky.

Mary Lynn and I play dead.

Rabbi Susie is the only sister who's married with children. *From left to right:* Aliza, Hallell, Adar, Zamir, and Ashira.

My nephew Zamir shortly after he was adopted from Ethiopia. He didn't know any English yet, but the bit Jimmy and I were doing still KILLED.

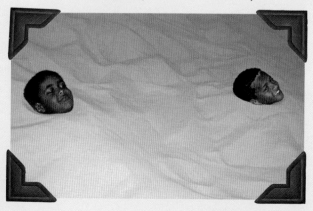

My nephews, Zamir and Adar, demanded to be buried in the sand, though it came out looking a tad race crime-y.

An appearance on the cable access show *Colin's Sleazy Friends*. I wrote a song *(facing page)* for this porn actress, Tiffany Millions *(pictured to the right of me)*, and later performed it in *Jesus Is Magic*.

A benefit held at the Playboy mansion. I did stand-up after an auction in which they sold everything from a five-day, all-expenses-paid golf vacation to this woman who offered to "go down on your wife while you watch." She asked to have her picture taken with me. I like that she's naked but with a purse.

There are special
toilets for girls like
you
~~There~~ it goes down
~~~~ to flush your pee
And then squirts up
to clean the poo

There's a dream in your
head
That'll never come true
              stickiness all over
There's a ~~head~~ ~~~~
~~~~ ~~dried up poo~~
~~from gangbang cumshots~~
~~shot~~
And it didn't come from you

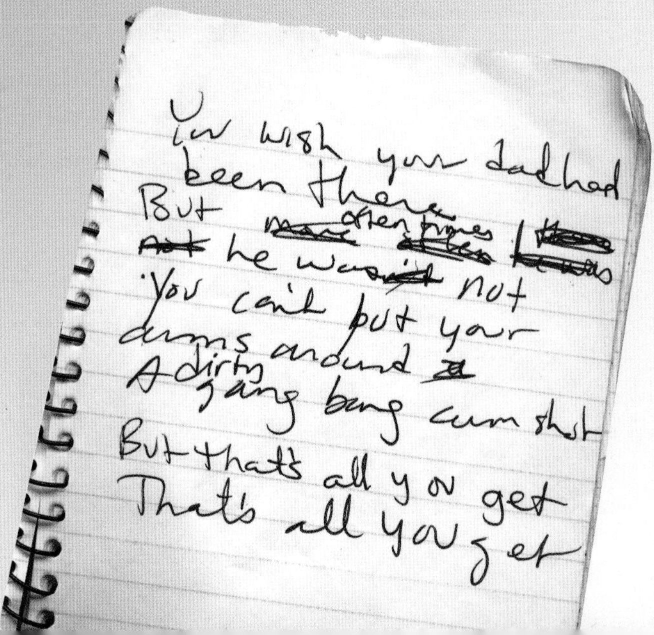

I wish your dad had
been there
But ~~~~ often times ~~~~
~~And~~ he was not
You can't put your
arms around ~~it~~
A dirty gang bang cum shot
But that's all you get
That's all you get

My dog, Duck. (His name is Doug on the show—it was a stoned whim and now I'm stuck with it.) He's almost sixteen years old and nearly died last year. It was so scary but now he's GREAT, though he needs at least twenty-two hours of sleep or he's not himself.

The cast of *TSSP*: Jay Johnston, Brian Posehn, guest star Patton Oswalt, Steve Agee, Laura Silverman, and me, on a break while shooting on the street.

The one time I get to meet a president and my hair looks like THIS.

The day after Jimmy and I broke up, my dad e-mailed this picture to me saying that he loved me and asking if I was okay. It actually really cheered me up, if only for the fact that I know he had to go to the "Effects" panel to make it this very sympathetic sepia tone.

I went to the Democratic National Convention in Denver and forgot I still had a pot cookie in my backpack. Just as it hit me, I was introduced to Al Gore. I'm not sure what I'm saying to him here but I think it's something to the effect of, "ARRRGGHH! I'm a monster!! I'm gonna eat you!"

Sell The Vatican, Feed The World (HD, Official)

Tour Vatican and Rome
choose from 70 private and group tours with expert guides, no lines
www.VaticanToursInc.com

Ads by Google

0:15 / 2:59

This is a still from my video *Sell the Vatican, Feed the World*. Notice the advertisement attached to this YouTube viewing.

A monkey dressed as a bellhop.
Classic . . .

mentioned that he liked *The Great Schlep* (a video I did telling Jewish kids to make their Floridian grandparents vote Obama), which was nice. It's amazing to think that the shocking, irreverent hero I once knew was now traveling with bodyguards and an entourage. It was probably a good thing I stabbed him in the head back then, and not now.

Chris Farley Unwittingly Changes My Life Forever

My stint at *SNL* was quick and painful. One might even compare it metaphorically to being stabbed in the head with a pencil. But it was a singular experience that I wouldn't trade. And there was at least one moment that continues to have a positive effect on my mental health on a daily basis.

Chris Farley and I had gotten to rehearsal early. We sat side by side, legs dangling off the edge of the main stage of the studio. "Can you believe this?" he asked. "Can you believe we're sitting on the same stage that John Belushi and Dan Aykroyd were on? *Performing* on the same stage they *performed* on?" He teemed with all the excitement and thrill and wonder that *I* should have had as a first-year *SNL*-er. So far from jaded—something he never seemed to become—Chris was downright awestruck, even three years into his tenure at *SNL*, in the thick of becoming a comedy legend.

I was taken aback by Chris's ability to be so earnest and joyful. Me, I'd been too gripped by fear to feel anything else. This quiet, coincidental moment with Chris made me realize, "I'd better feel this, *now*," and it remains a kind of mantra for me. This was surely not a defining moment for Chris—he was most likely passing the time, filling in an awkward encounter with a newbie with some friendly words, but it meant the world to me and has made the rest of my life a better place. And it's because of him that I now sit on the set of my own TV show between takes and yell, "You guys!! Can you believe this?? We're making a real TV show!! This is going to be on motherfucking TELEVISION!" They laugh at me, but I mean it. It's a joy.

FEAR AND CLOTHING

I have a little problem.

It's one I've had for quite a while, and it is not mellowing with age. In fact, by all accounts it's getting worse.

I don't know how to dress myself.

That's not *my* opinion, it's the opinion of those who matter most in America: the editors of *Us Weekly* magazine. Someday after I die, my fashion style will be reevaluated, and I will be seen as a genius like all dead people. But from the day God gave me my own self-generating fur coat, I have pretty much been a perpetual fashion "don't."

To make sure that I would not be exaggerating my claims of persecution here, I did what any diligent person who does not wish to get out of her chair would do: I Googled myself using my name plus "worst dressed" as search terms, and got over 18,000 hits. As a control, I then Googled my name with "*best* dressed" and still wound up with about 18,000 hits, so I figured it was a wash. But then I looked closer at the "Best Dressed" results and saw such entries as "Best Cinderella's Ugly Step Sister: Sarah Silverman." Once you start getting sarcastic Google search results, you know irony has truly bled into all areas of modern American life.

Suspenders of Disbelief

I'm pretty much fine with the way I dress, so I don't see my style as a personal flaw. But if you do, and are looking for someone to blame, try my parents. My father to this day refuses to wear anything with a label other than "Target" (he has three collared shirts in rotation, which he ordered online from the Target employees' Web site), and my mother, for example, might don overalls with two different color socks—the latter being pure artistic choice, not slapdashery. I pretty much followed suit. Though once I entered my teen years, I started wanting the latest in New Hampshire trendiness; until then, clothing was to me a way to keep warm and express my interests and passions.

One of my biggest interests and passions, at age ten, was Mork. From Ork. So when I went to Camp Forevergreen that summer, I brought my favorite (and only) fashion accessory: my rainbow Mork-from-Ork suspenders. It was my firm understanding that these were the coolest things a kid could own. But as it turns out, they were not cool in the least. What they were, in actuality, was an invitation to torment me. Abby Rothschild, a tough, towheaded bunkmate twice my size, was the first to accept.

One morning as we prepared to go on a hike, she cooed, "Sarah, you should wear your rainbow suspenders. They're soooo coool." To my gullible ears, Abby sounded sincere, and generally speaking, it did not take much coaxing for me to break out the Morkwear.

When we left the bunk, I was proudly sporting the suspenders over a yellow collared Forevergreen shirt.

Not long into the hike I noticed that no matter how slowly I paced myself, Abby and her friends remained a few feet behind me, cackling with delight. Eventually I stopped and turned around to find out what was so funny, at which point the girls stifled their giggles. That was my answer.

"Did you tell me to wear these because they're gay?!" I asked Abby. At first she and her pals just looked at me, startled. Then they cracked up again, and I did too. Genuinely.

"I can't help it—*I fucking love Mork!*" I said. And kept laughing. Joining in their laughter saved me then. It continues to save me now.

After that hike, Abby Rothschild became my best friend and biggest protector. She did confess that she hated my guts when I sang "A Bicycle Built for Two" at the camp talent show, and that to her I'd always be a fucking gaylord. But she thought that I sang pretty good and, besides, I was funny.

My mom, beautiful, in overalls

It Is Brought to My Attention That I Am Scum

A bby and I remained friends outside of camp. She lived in a very affluent town in Massachusetts called Lynnfield. For my first weekend visit to the Rothschilds', I arrived in my hometown uniform of Levi's and a denim coat. No matter how cold the weather got, in Manchester, New Hampshire, your winter jacket is jean.

Abby and I were so excited to see each other. She showed me her room and her stuff and her friends, and since she already knew I wet the bed, there were no secrets. My mom had already talked to Abby's about waking me up to pee. But something didn't seem quite right; I got the feeling that Abby's mom was unsure about me, and I had never felt this before—parents generally loved me. The Christian adults in my very Christian town usually held me up to their kids as a model Jew. And though I was used to being regarded as different at home with the "Jew" thing and all, here in Lynnfield there had to be something else creating this sense that somehow I didn't fit in. I got a distinct vibe from Mrs. Rothschild—like she thought I was going to steal something. It made me extra well behaved. I was too nervous to even be sassy or silly. And then just before we got in the car to go to lunch, she cornered Abby and under her breath—with teeth clenched—I heard her say,

"Abby, tell her."

Shrugging, Abby turned to me and said apologetically,

"Only scumbags wear jean jackets."

I was stunned. I didn't have a mom who would refer to little kids as "scumbags." I wasn't sure how to respond. I just looked at Abby and her mom, and said, "Oh, okay." I traded in my jean jacket, the one I had silk-screened on the back "The Beatles, Let It Be" during industrial arts class—you know, as only a scumbag would do—for a more Lynnfield appropriate coat, supplied by Abby and her wonderful mother. I wore it the rest of the weekend.

Abby's Bat Mitzvah. From right to left (Hebrew-style): Me, Abby, unknown Jewess. Notice my occasion-appropriate attire.

The One Time I Should Have Said Yes to a Group of Guys Who Wanted Me to Remove My Dress

One morning in the summer of '09, I woke up and saw that I had six voice-mail messages. My heart sank—I was sure someone had died. But they were messages of congratulations. I'd been nominated for an Emmy in the category of Lead Actress in a Comedy Series. It was a thrill and a complete shock. The show hadn't been on the air in several months, and seemed so off the radar compared to its competition. We were in production on our new season and the possibility of Emmy recognition crossed none of our minds—so much so that we weren't even aware when the nomination announcements were made.

I knew there was less than a zero percent chance I would actually win. The nomination was already such a huge victory to me, so I looked forward to the Emmys with little anxiety.

As if the Emmy thing wasn't cool enough, this superfancy design house, Badgley Mischka, offered to make me a dress for the occasion. I'm not generally a fancy-gown kind of girl, but this night was special. *Make-It-a-Treat* special. I wanted to look like a princess.

I picked out the satiny fabric and the cobalt blue color, then Badgley Mischka sent over a basic template, along with a local tailor named Yuliy Mosk who would help me make tweaks to it, since BM (tee hee—BM . . .) is located in New York. I went crazy with the tweaks—it was fun to kind of be the designer, to turn it into something that was truly my own creation. It was becoming the most beautiful dress ever.

At one of the last fittings, Yuliy seemed very nervous.

"Yuliy? Are you okay?"

"I have to tell you something," he said, gravely.

I couldn't imagine what fashiony thing could possibly be so worrisome.

Yuliy said, "I sent the picture of the final dress to the designers, and . . . well . . . they're opting to take their name off the dress."

Truthfully, I didn't care. I'm not into the glamour of fancy designer names and haute couture shows. I thought I totally understood—this creation didn't look like the conservative kind of dress they made. It had become something else entirely. Something crazy *awesome*, that is! I did not falter in thinking this was the prettiest dress in the world. I told Yuliy, "I'm so happy now that when people ask who made this dress, I can say, 'Yuliy Mosk!'" I took Yuliy's lack of response as an expression of modesty and humble gratitude.

On Emmy night, I strolled onto the red carpet preening with confidence, feeling radiant, swirling and twirling around like a Semitic Cinderella. I even think my voice was different—like, I was even *talking* like a princess. And I proudly beamed Yuliy's name at every interview.

"This is a collaboration with the great designer Yuliy Mosk! And look! It has pockets!"

I *inched* down the red carpet, giving everyone with a camera their chance. I stood there, flashbulbs popping, imagining the imminent comments over my fashion triumph, *The real victory tonight was not in the form of a statuette, but rather it hung on the comely frame of a certain actress-comedienne . . .*

And then the next day came.

I got on the Web. I Googled "Sarah Silverman" "Emmys" "dress." I didn't need to see reader comments—only pictures of myself—to realize that I looked like a fucking crazy blue house, or more specifically like a crazy person in some kind of small-town community-theater performance, who was *playing* a house. The dress was bizarrely wide, loose-fitting, and built to look like I possibly had some kind of elephantitis of my lower half. What the hell happened? On Emmy night, everyone around me seemed to really like the dress, but then again, what were they gonna say? "Welcome to the biggest night of your professional life. Are you a monster from the last Star Wars movie?"

After studying the crime scene photos, I can see at least one place I really went off the rails in the design process. In the early fittings, I'd told Yuliy to loosen the corset. He was uneasy about the idea, to say the least, but I insisted. I was gonna be at the Emmys all night, and I didn't want to be uncomfortable. But as it happens, there's no such thing as a "boyfriend corset" for a reason. The whole point of corsets is that they have to be supertight. They are made to crush your ribs and thus change your silhouette—that's part of it. But even though I don't drink, I have full-on beer goggles when it comes to things that, by any other set of eyes, look fucking embarrassingly terrible on me. Case in point:

Sarah Silverman swallowed by 2009 Emmy dress.

Sarah Silverman made waves at Sunday night's Emmy Awards in Los Angeles with her traffic stopping red carpet look. Big . . . blue . . . tsunami like waves of some sort of fabric popularized by the designers at David's Bridal.

While Sarah Silverman offered up one of the truly intentionally funny moments of the 2009 Emmy Awards with her mustache gag, nothing could obscure the hidiocy of the gown which looked like a sort of royal blue satin octopus swallowing Sarah Silverman from the bottom up.

Unfortunately, evil genius Sarah Silverman also provided some unintentional comedy moments during her appearance on the Emmy Awards red carpet. Sarah wore a royal blue strapless gown that looked like it was swiped from the fat girl in class who wanted to buy a dress that she could wear to both the junior prom and the Renn Faire wedding she has coming up later this summer to coincide with the harvest season. The dress was both ill-fitting and drape-ish.

Eh, what can I say? I'm a comfort-is-key kind of person, and,
corny as it sounds, the prettiest thing you can wear is a smile, and
when shit is too tight or my feet hurt or I'm cold, I'm just not happy.
I'm my parents' daughter. My mom with her overalls, my dad with
his stained sweatshirts from Target, and me with my baggy corset
and house-sized blue dress.

MIDWORD

H i. It's me, Sarah. How have you been enjoying the book so far?
Don't answer that.

I am about to do something revolutionary, something genius. I
hope you don't get queasy at the sight of trails being blazed, because
that's what's about to happen right before your eyes if you read any
further. As you may recall, I blew your mind on the very first page
of this book, with my self-written foreword, or what will now forever be known as an "auto-foreword." You've probably embarrassed
yourself already with audible "Oh my god"s on the subway. Strangers
have looked up from their Sudoku, wondering what you're gasping
at. Others have seen what you're reading and understand. *Dianetics* is
a fucking joke, a fairy tale. What you're about to read will take the
place of every religion's bible in terms of awesomeness.

Welcome. You are now reading literature's very first *midword*. Up
until now, there has been the *foreword* (and now the auto-foreword)
and, of course, the highly vaunted *afterword*, but it was always lim-
ited to those two. But why? Everything else has a middle. Stories
have them. Life has them. Relationships have them. We live in a

nation whose character is largely defined by its middle. The people who live in it, themselves, have large middles. I have read that, in economic terms, there's not much left of the middle class, but I think my thesis is still pretty strong: Things have middles.

What is a middle for? A middle is the same with pretty much anything. In anatomy, it's where nutrients are digested and broken down before their journey to the anus. In life, the middle is where everything that's happened thus far is reflected upon, spiritually digested if you will, and corrections are made based on this reflection.

And that's how the midword will serve in this book—and no doubt, all of the books that will soon be following this very precedent I am setting. It is now time to reflect. So here I go . . .

What I have learned thus far in writing this book is that writing this book is a gigantic pain in the ass. It's long and it's lonely and I already know most of what I'm telling you. In some moments, this shit is flat-out depressing. Whose jackass idea was it for me to write a book anyway? I'm a comedian. Comedians are almost universally tortured, and not even redeemed like normal writers are by being "deep."

I've quickly learned that the best way to write a book is to frequently stop writing your book and reward yourself for every tiny parcel of progress. Or if you're not making any progress, stop and reward yourself for having tried. I like this system a lot because all day long I'm rewarding myself. I don't know if it will lead to an actual book, but that's not really what it's about in the end, is it? Here's a short list of things I've done while not writing this book:

I Googled myself.

I started watching Damages *and* Law & Order, Criminal Intent, *the latter which, luckily, is on at almost all times.*

I learned how to use Garage Band and then wrote and recorded a tween heartbreak song which I decided I would give to Miley Cyrus or Selena Gomez or Taylor Swift.

I exercised—which almost got me to write instead.

I Googled myself.

I bought a ukelele and learned how to play "Amazing Grace," "Bill Bailey, Won't You Please Come Home," "Clementine," and "When the Saints Go Marching In."

I convinced myself my dog had a fever.

I found a mole. It's on the left side of my lower back. My left.

I fell into a deep post-Googling nap.

I bought eleven separate pieces of apparel from bluefly.com, chickdowntown .com, and eluxury.com, and returned all but one. A hat.

I cut the tops off several pair of American Apparel tube socks and made them into striped wrist affectations.

I bought vitamins that stimulate brain function.

I bought vitamins that tell your brain when you are full.

I bought vitamins that build immune systems inside you.

I bought "fat-burning lemonade."

I spent hours at Staples.

I went to lunch with friends.

I met friends for coffee.

I met friends for breakfast.

I called my parents to catch up.

I Skyped with my friend Heidi and lectured her about doing something with her life.

I smoked pot to help the creative juices flow, which resulted in looking way too closely in the mirror, being disgusted, taking pictures of my breasts in awkward but flattering positions to e-mail to a manboy I've been seeing, mixing odd combinations of kitchen cabinet remnants and finding them "fucking unbelievably delicious" and then falling asleep, face unwashed.

It's shocking to discover that writing a book is mostly an exercise in masturbation. Not literary masturbation—*literal* masturbation. Every other hour, you're getting up from your desk and going to your bed. I'm actually pleased with the previous two sentences—they were pretty funny. In fact, they deserve a reward of some kind . . .

*   *   *

. . . Okay, I'm back. Here's a weird thing that's freaking me out right now: I think I've reached the middle of the midword. Is this something I need to acknowledge or deal with? Based on everything I was saying before, it might be. But not entirely sure. This is all new territory. Hopefully my successors in midword writing—and I'm telling you there will be many—will straighten this all out.

*   *   *

So guess what just happened: I came up with the title of my book, and it was approved by HarperCollins. This may not seem exciting to you, but you don't understand what a fucking hassle the whole thing has been. They scoffed at "My Life in 18 Poops." And to say they were underwhelmed by "Tales of a Horse-Faced Jew-Monkey" would be like saying that Hitler was underwhelmed by the Jews. It was reviled at every rung of the corporate ladder. More alternate titles pitched by me and my various friends include: "Reflections on the Global Century Plus Farts"; "Straight from the Horse-ish Mouth"; "Sarah Silverman: I Said 'Vagina,' Now Make Me Famous." But finally, as you now do, they love and admire, "The Bedwetter: Stories of Courage, Redemption, and Pee."

Anyway, today we finally agreed on that title, which was an enormous relief. But there was one last battle. It was over the *subtitle*, and

it was a doozy. To refresh your memory, the subtitle is "Stories of Courage, Redemption, and Pee." With HarperCollins's permission, I provide the e-mail exchange below (this is 100 percent real, by the way), between my editor, David Hirshey, and me:

From: Hirshey, David

Sent: Wednesday, August 26, 2009 8:29 AM
To: 'Sarah'

For what it's worth, I've always preferred pee-pee to pee. Ask anyone.

From: Sarah Silverman

Sent: Wednesday, August 26, 2009 12:14 PM
To: Hirshey, David
Subject: Re: This just in

Excellent—though I stand strong with just Pee

On Aug 26, 2009, at 11:58 AM, "Hirshey, David" wrote:

With all due respect, I think you're wrong on this. Pee doesn't work. The rhythm is off. Pee is vaguely unpleasant, pee-pee is funny.

From: Sarah

Sent: Wednesday, August 26, 2009 3:47 PM
To: Hirshey, David
Subject: Re: The Great Pee-Pee vs. Pee Debate

Pee is the only option. With all due respect.

On Aug 26, 2009, at 4:45 PM, "Hirshey, David" wrote:

Hey Sarah—

I hear you but I'm also trying to balance the concerns of our Marketing and Sales gurus who are not measuring the subtitle in humor calories. They just want it to sell. And they feel that "pee-pee" is far better because it sounds "childlike and playful." One guy estimated that pee vs. pee-pee could mean the difference of tens of thousands of copies sold, which is not insignificant. So I hope you can see it from both sides.

David

----- Original Message -----

From: Sarah Silverman
To: Hirshey, David
Sent: Wed, Aug 26, 2009 6:28 pm
Subject: The Great Pee-Pee vs. Pee Debate

This is fucking retarded and based on nothing but hang ups of people I dont know. Pee is simple and clean and pee-pee is something you say in a baby voice which I find gross and would never say. This may be based on MY hang ups, but better mine than some faceless douche's.

I am actually gonna die on this hill.

On Aug 27, 2009, at 8:05 AM, "Hirshey, David" wrote:

I now know that "pee" stands for passion and in this case your passion has won out. Pee it is! I hope you understand that I was just trying to mediate among all the corporate voices in the building as well as honor your vision for the book. But it's your book and if you like "pee," then I'm sitting down with that.

And that was pretty much that. Pretty much, except there was one more noteworthy missive. It was not one I was supposed to read, but as so often happens in the lives of busy professionals, people forward things by mistake, or deliberately forward whole e-mails that they had intended to edit before sending. Here's one such between my editor and his über-boss . . .

From: Hirshey, David

Sent: Friday, August 28, 2009 11:51 AM
To: Morrison, Michael

As you know, I'm scheduled to leave Tuesday for LA to "supervise" the cover shoot for Sarah's book and we still haven't agreed on a subtitle and cover concept. I'll spare you the blizzard of e-mails with Madame Silverman about the cover of her book but suffice it to say she ground me down on the title. I wanted to push it over the line and call it "The Kikerunner."
Sarah, while patronizingly conceding that "it's kinda funny," dismissed it not for taste reasons but for commerical concerns.
"I'll never be able to say the title of the book on TV," she said quite reasonably.
"Couldn't you have fun with it and say 'It rhymes with Bikerunner'?"
"I also don't want people to think I wrote a parody of an international best-seller and movie that came out five years ago."
So we settled on her title that is "kinda funny" in a confessional sort of way: "The Bedwetter" It's certainly a lot better than her original title: "Tales From A Horse-Faced Jew Monkey," so we're ahead on that score.
Then came the surreal battle over the subtitle. We agreed on everything but the last word "Stories of Courage, Redemption and TK." I wanted the last word to be "Pee-pee" because I felt it was funnier and less off-putting than "Pee."

Ok, now I think I fold.

I share the above exchanges with you because they're representative of what most of my days are like. At any given moment, I'm mired in some sort of surreal teleconference or e-mail debate. I'll be arguing with late-night TV producers over the merits of "Chink" versus "dirty Jew," or clawing at the MTV Networks Standards and Practices Department, which oversees my TV show, for permission to say the words "labia" or "gaping rectum." I am in a frequent state of exasperation, but I also kind of love this about my life.

And that's about it for the midword. And now, please enjoy the rest of this delightful romp I like to call *my book*.

EXPLOSIVE DIARY

I've heard that when one writes in a diary, they are secretly hoping that it will someday be read and appreciated by others. But have you actually ever read anyone's diary? I doubt it, because they are unreadable. If life is a meal, then diaries are the toilets in which we shit out its vile remnants. They are litanies of complaints, grandiosity, and self-pity. There's always the occasional happy entry, but they tend to be more brief. If my experience with this book is any guide, the very act of sitting alone in a room writing fuels misery. If you're happy, you probably don't have time to write for long periods in a diary because you're out barbecuing or doing some sort of fusion-y sport like surf-ball-skiing or heli-yoga-jumping—I'm pretty sure this is what chronically happy people are up to. Regardless of the tone of the entries, what diaries never contain is an interesting story—which I recall my English professor from NYU saying is what people actually like to read. Behold this entry from an actual fourteen-year-old girl's diary:

Today was fine. I think I'm starting to become friends with Tara Atta. She's really nice. Julie is downright cruel. Uhhg! She makes me so frus-

trated. I get so paralyzed around her. I feel like she's saying things about me behind my back. I really think she is. It makes me feel so helpless. Oh well, as Dad says, "This too shall pass."

But wait—look how much more boring it is when she's *not* depressed:

Today was fine. It seems kind of weird, I've been having not boring really, but very ordinary days lately. I'm starting a book called "The Color Purple." It is excellent. I find it hard to put down. My mother bought it for herself to read because both of my sisters read it and said it was a great book.

The only way this diary entry would be interesting is if this little girl had turned out to be Oprah Winfrey, who starred in the movie *The Color Purple.* But she didn't turn out to be Oprah Winfrey. She turned out to be some Jewy comedian reputed to have an unhealthy obsession with penises, vaginas, and farts.

Occasionally, I had a gem in there (if I do say so myself). I enjoy this one:

I was practicing the song I'm singing on Saturday and mom was telling me I should add all these motions in. I thought they were fairly odd and told her so, and she then said quite seriously, "Yeah, well you don't know your ass from your elbow." I didn't know what to say next, so I put my hand over my elbow and told my mother I had to go to the bathroom. At least I made her laugh, but I was still steamed at her.

But occasional jokes in my diaries are drowned in an ocean of crap like this:

Today wasn't that great. I was totally deppressed [sic] all day (actually from about 3:45–7:20, but it seemed much longer). I was so sad and it seemed like no one understood how I felt! When I really thought about it, I think part of the reason that I was upset was because I feel like such a baby! Especially since Jody is only 3 months older than me and she is almost total [sic] self-reliant. And it's not anyone else's fault. I think they treat me my age. It's just me. I don't know what's wrong with me. I'm such a baby. I can't keep myself company. I really need someone w/ me at just about all times.

At first glance you might find the above interesting but that's because it's *me*, and you obviously find me interesting enough to read this book. But try reading five more entries like that and soon you will want a time machine so you can travel back to the mid-'80s, find me as a tween, and rip that pen out of my hand. Incidentally, if you're going to be doing this, could you also swing by my place in the fall of '94 and prevent me from getting naked with a guy named Roger Borsky? I have never fully recovered from the smell of that man's balls.

I believe that diary entries are not written to be read. They're written to be *written* and then to be put in a drawer, eventually to be discovered by one's grandchild after one's death. At which point the kid will say, "Wow, I cannot wait to learn more about my grandparent by reading her diary entries, I bet they are fascinating." At that juncture, the grandchild will put the old diary in a box and go off to live her own life of self-created drama and, finally, will set pen to paper of her own diary, thinking she's commemorating the great drama of her life, when in reality she's recording only the most boring aspects of it. Unvisited tombstones, unread diaries, and erased video-game high-score rankings are three of the most potent symbols of mankind's pathetic and fruitless attempts at immortality. Not to be negative.

Ultimately, diaries are to writing what masturbation is to sex. The thoughts and fantasies that go through one's mind wind up in a tangible form, either on a sheet of paper or a sheet on your bed, and they should be quietly disposed of.

I should say that I'm mostly talking about the diaries of teenage girls. Teenage boys' diaries are different. They tend to read thusly:

> Dear Diary:
>
> I've been feeling so—oh, oops, look at this, I'm writing in a diary. So I guess that settles it: I'm gay. Thanks, Diary!

As an exercise before tackling this chapter, I tried writing my first diary entry as an actual grown-up, with an appropriately adult sense of perspective and balance. Here's how it turned out:

> Today was okay. Having fun writing my book, but running out of things to say. Wish I'd been raped or something. That's at least a chapter. Mackenzie Phillips is so lucky. Why couldn't I have had sex with my father? I guess for one thing he made his living selling women's clothing and I don't see myself with someone in retail. But also because to do that is really bad form. It's just that MP's book is selling like proverbial hotcakes (poss fun/jokey piece for my book: try to compile evidence which proves that hotcakes never sold especially well) and that gratification alone probably mitigates whatever psychic damage was there from the teenage incest and heroin addiction. Wonder if it's too late for something like this to happen to me—some sort of horrible tragedy, but one that doesn't permanently disfigure me? Poss scenarios: me on run from mob, witness protection program, having to wear wacky but flattering disguises; me with some sort of serious addiction, but to something that doesn't age my skin. Moisturizer addiction? Eh. Addicted to sex with Clive Owen.

Needless to say, the exercise proved my theory: It's impossible to write a good diary entry. I mean, do you see what I'm talking about? There's no storytelling in the above whatsoever.

I began to get depressed.

I strive to be a healthy, self-aware, fully actualized woman, and it seemed to me that reading what I wrote as a child was a critical step along the path to understanding myself. But there was just no fucking way I could read that garbage. Life is too short to be immersed in drab, repetitive prose that goes nowhere. I called my editor at HarperCollins and got a referral for a professional writer who could "punch up" my diary entries. Someone who could extract the compelling parts and put them in a more entertaining framework. Here's a sample of the results:

> "Today was okay," Sarah intoned to herself quietly, as her skin pulsed with the glowing warmth from her fireplace, which broke the silence only now and then with crisp consonants from the microscopic explosions of immolating timber, procured at local almond groves.
>
> She began to reflect on her burgeoning friendship with Tara Atta. Would Tara ultimately disappoint her, as Julie had? Who was Tara Atta, really? And who was she to Sarah? Had they any genuine mutual admiration, or tangible emotional connection? Or were they merely two desperate voices in the squall of teenage life, calling to each other in terror and in hope, like survivors of a remote mountain avalanche? Could it be that this described all human relationships?

Okay, was this asshole kidding me? He put it in *third person*. Who writes their diary like that? I had to spend hours replacing all the pronouns. In general, though, I really liked it. The avalanche metaphor was killer, and then the way he wondered if love and friendship was all just about people finding ports in a storm—that's exactly

the type of stuff I think about. I highly recommend this guy to anyone who strives to learn more about themselves but cannot actually
stand themselves.

But unreadable prose is not the most shameful result of keeping
a diary. It's also an extended lesson in becoming a stalker. Little
girls spend their childhood composing countless passionate letters
to a recipient who never once writes them back. Which gives me a
great idea, by the way. I'm going to invent something, and by the
time my as-yet-unconceived daughter is old enough to be slather-
ing self-pity all over the pages of her diary, it will exist. And it will
change not only her life but the lives of all young women and gay
boys. I'll call it "The Smart Diary." It will be computerized, and
the software will be designed so that every time the diarist adds an
entry, my device will write her back! But "The Smart Diary" won't
coddle its scribe or tolerate the standard self-indulgence. Here's an
example of what I'm imagining:

> SARAH: *Today wasn't that great. I was totally deppressed [sic] all day (actu-
> ally from about 3:45–7:20, but it seemed <u>much</u> longer). I was <u>so</u> sad
> and it seemed like no one understood how I felt!*

> DIARY: *I hear you. You remind me so much of another Jewish teenager who kept
> a diary. She lived in an attic in Amsterdam and never knew the joy of
> rainbow parties or sexting. And she never complained.*

> SARAH: *Today was fine. It seems kind of weird, I've been having not boring
> really, but very ordinary days lately.*

> DIARY: *Oops, can you repeat that last entry? I fell asleep two words in.
> I have this odd habit of losing consciousness whenever subjected to mind-
> blowing boredom.*

> SARAH: *. . . I don't know what's wrong with me. I'm such a baby. I can't keep
> myself company. I really need someone w/me at just about all times.*

DIARY: *Wow! Is this diary entry based on the book* Push *by Sapphire?*

3/17/85 -Dry-

Today was fine.
(For a Sunday.) I
was home alone
for a while and
then dad came
once and we went
for a walk, played
catch and went to
pick up Janice and
then he dropped me
back off. I got ready
to go to rehearsal
(Nun Hazon) and
the Barnard's picked
me up.
Bye
— Sarah Silverman

3/18/85   -Wet-

Today was fine.
I think I'm starting
to become friends
with Tarra Atta. She's
really nice. Julie
is downright cruel. Uh ho
She makes me so frust-
rated. I get so paranoy
around her. I feel
like she's saying
things about me
behind my back
I really think
she is. It makes me
feel so helpless
Oh well, as dad
says, "This too will
pass."
— By Sarah Silverman

2/6/85 -Dry-

Today was fine. It
seems kind of weird,
I've been having not
boring really, but very
ordinary days lately. I'm
starting a book called
"The Color Purple." It is
excellent. I find it
hard to put down. My
mother bought it
for herself to read
because both of
my sisters read it
and said it was
a great book. Mom
and I are reading
it at →

the same time,
so I don't get to
read it whenever I
want, because she
finds it hard to put
down too! Tomorrow
I'm sleeping over Dads.
I'm not really nervous.
I don't know why I
hesitate going there. I
love it, I mean, I don't
want to be just try-
ing to convince my-
self of that, but I
seem to be okay once
I'm there.
    I love Rosie
so much. It
sometimes →

I've shared the foregoing thoughts not as an attack on the very notion of keeping a diary, but as a plea—a plea from a woman who has learned from brutal experience. I signed a contract to write a book, the one you're reading, which is largely a reflection on my past. It would have been literary malpractice to have ignored my own diary entries, considering that they reflect what really happened in my past as opposed to how I'd like to remember it, so I read them. They were informative, and even amusing at moments, but by and large they bored and depressed the shit out of me.

As you write in your diary tonight, ask yourself, "Is this something that will be interesting in thirty years? Is this something that will be interesting tomorrow? To whom will it be interesting?

Once you've taken the time to answer these questions, very slowly turn around. I'm behind you!

ME PLAY JOKE

Dirty Jew Drops "Nigger,"
Picks "Chink" over "Spic"

T he second-worst disaster in American history preceded the first by exactly two months to the day. On July 11, 2001, I appeared on *Late Night with Conan O'Brien*. Although you wouldn't know it by looking on my imdb page (imdb.com is a Web site used throughout the entertainment industry to quickly reference people's professional credits; it's updated constantly, and it's very accurate; I have no idea how it happens or who does this), it's not listed there. It's as if this gig never happened.

The day that never happened went like this:

I arrive at 30 Rock and meet with Frank, the segment producer, to go over the plan. He tells me there's a problem with one of my jokes. The joke goes like this:

> *I got a jury duty form in the mail, and I don't wanna do jury duty. So my friend said, "Write something really racist on the form so they won't pick you, like 'I hate niggers.'" I was like, Jeez—I don't want people to think I'm racist, I just wanna get out of jury duty. So I filled out the form and I wrote "I love niggers."*

Frank says I can't say "nigger" on the show, even though it's obviously not a racist joke, it's a joke about an idiot—me—trying to get out of jury duty. But no way could that word be uttered on NBC—period. "What about saying 'the N word'?" Frank suggests, but I tell him that won't work. It has to be brutal. "The N word" is the opposite of brutal; it's the phrase one uses when being delicate. He tries again: "What about substituting *'dirty Jew'*?" At first I like the idea, but decide that because I actually *am* Jewish, it would dilute the humor. The more offensive the hate word, the more sharply it highlights the idiocy of the speaker.

So I say, "Nah. 'Dirty Jew' makes it too soft since I *am* a dirty Jew. How about 'Chink'?"

"No," Frank says. "How about 'Spic'? You can say 'Spic.'"

"How come I can say 'Spic' and not 'Chink'? That doesn't make sense. Fuck that—if I can say 'Spic' then I can say 'Chink.' I'm saying 'Chink'—it's a funnier-sounding word."

He doesn't argue. "Chink" it is.

I go out and sit on the couch with Conan to do the show. It turns out great. The joke about jury duty gets huge laughs. I go home to my sublet in the Village, feeling pleased with myself.

An Asian American Man Expresses the Wish That I Burn in Hell. My Mother Expresses the Wish That I Wear Jewelry.

The next morning I woke up to my cell phone ringing. I couldn't get to it before voice-mail picked up, but I saw the caller ID—it was Mom.

"Hi, Honey, it's Mom. I was just watching *The View* and they were talking about you! They said that some guy from an Asian American watchdog group is very upset that you said 'Chink' and wants an apology, and then Lisa Ling agreed that that word is racist, and they played the clip from last night of you on *Conan* and you looked GORGEOUS! But I really wish you would wear earrings. Earrings always frame a face . . ."

I was in shock. I went online and found the man my mother was talking about. His name was Guy Aoki, and he was from the Media Action Network for Asian Americans, or MANAA.

I felt terrible that he was upset and wanted to explain myself, so I found Guy's e-mail address on his Web site and wrote him a long message. I really worked hard on it, too. I enlisted my sister Susan, who's a rabbi, and her husband—he's a super-Jew with the super-Jewiest of names, Yosef Israel Abramowitz—to help me craft this e-mail just right.

Amazingly, for someone like me, who could lose a priceless Fabergé egg seconds after possessing it, my manager actually saved what I wrote. It appears here on the following page . . .

Reading this now, I wince at how my self-righteousness seems to match his. I received a very short, curt response from him that I wish I'd saved, but didn't. He also gave out my e-mail address to all the members of MANAA, and I wish he hadn't, because I received pages and pages of hate mail every day for months. You might think I'd just change my e-mail address, but you would be wrong. I can withstand almost anything if it means I can avoid tedious tasks. It's pretty impressive that to this day—eight years later—I still use that same e-mail address. I guess you could say I'm lazier than a . . . Eh, skip it.

To: Guy Aoki, President
Media Action Network for Asian Americans
From: Sarah Silverman, Comedian
7/18/01

Dear Guy--

I heard that you were hurt by my joke on the Conan O'Brien show, and wanted to write to you and address it. I had no intention to offend. The joke is satirical and the intended point of view is to underline the ignorance people demonstrate when they employ racial epithets. In my act, the joke is usually in a greater context, which explores race, tolerance, and fear.

I would like to say, though, that any notion I have of success does not just come from the laughter I hear, but the source of that laughter. If I had an all-white fanbase, I would re-evaluate my material, but because it is multi-ethnic, I feel as though the interpretation of my material is, for the most part, as intended.

Some people react to buzz-words before listening to the context of those words. Isn't that ignorance?

A storm has brewed in the wake of my appearance on The Conan O'Brien Show in which I used a derogatory slur for Chinese and other Asian people. You demanded an apology and received it from NBC, who also promised to edit my piece out of repeats of that show. I believe you have not served well the cause of rooting out racism.

I am grateful to people, like yourself, who dedicate their selves to naming and making public the bigotry that they see. As a comedian, I use irony, often playing the role of ignoramus—like in the Conan piece in question--to turn the public eye toward the bigotry that goes unnoticed. The subtext is clearly in direct contrast to the text. It is ironic humor, and I see it as part of a larger effort - the same effort of which you are part.

In this case, you reacted to a buzz-word without paying attention to its context.

It is unfortunate, then, when the first reaction to an incident of suspected bigotry is to name an enemy and make demands. In this world-view, you have cast me as the bigot to your victim. I would have loved to talk to you about this face-to-face. I believe that real change happens when people put their energies together--not just from a series of issued statements. Sometimes awareness can even be raised by a comic's silly routine.

You have garnered millions of dollars in free publicity with the exploitation of my joke. I would have preferred to talk seriously and honestly about how to address the real challenges to a good society. We obviously have different approaches to addressing racism. Certainly, that should not make us enemies.

I apologize for the pain I've unintentionally caused you. Even if it was unintentional, even if it was the result of a misinterpretation.

On an ongoing basis, I make it a practice to talk to people regarding the impact of my material and am grateful for your input.

The Conan O'Brien show is great because they don't pull punches for any ethnic group. Speaking as a Jew (another group that is often an "easy target") I appreciate their willingness to make fun and illuminate what is buried yet very present in our social unconscious.

Sincerely,
Sarah Silverman

After doing the *Conan* show, I flew back to L.A. and met with my then-manager, Geoff Cheddy, a curly-haired Jew with a goofy smile. Geoff sat me down and started talking:

"I pitched you for an all-comedian *Fear Factor*."

"Are you fucking *kidding* me?? Do you know me at ALL?? In a million fucking years I wouldn't do—"

"They don't want you."

Suddenly, I wasn't feeling so cocky.

"They don't want me on *Fear Factor*??"

"They don't want you on NBC. At all."

I was devastated. *All* of NBC?

To be banished by an entire network is scary for a young comedian. It's not that I wanted, per se, to be cast on a show where you're forced to eat the maggot-filled rotting intestines of a dead yak, but when the people who cast the maggot-eating show don't *want* you, that's a whole new career low.

Geoff went on to tell me that NBC had already released an apology for my behavior. As soon as Aoki complained, the network released this statement: "The joke was clearly inappropriate and the fact that it was not edited by our standards and practices department was a mistake. We have reviewed our procedures to ensure such an incident does not reoccur and we will edit the joke out of any future repeats."

Wow. You can really tell that this message came straight from the network's heart, and it's not surprising. Of course mucky-mucks at NBC would be deeply dismayed and apologetic about my offensive joke and quick to apologize for it. After all, any network that shows people eating the maggot-filled rotting intestines of dead yaks—during primetime, no less—is a network devoted to the preservation of human dignity.

Back at my apartment I picked up a message from one of the

producers of *Politically Incorrect with Bill Maher,* inviting me to defend myself on the show; Guy Aoki would be on the panel. I accepted, having yet to learn that there is nothing more pointless, and nothing less funny, than defending your own material. My ignorance was about to end.

With No Awareness of the Irony, I Try to Redeem My Talk-Show Debacle by Appearing on a Talk Show

I arrived alone at Television City studios, but I had two comic friends on my guest list—Doug Benson and Brian Posehn. I was ushered past the greenroom where Guy Aoki was sitting. He had black pin-straight hair, cut in the exact bowl shape I had when I was five, and the same mustache I had till I was fifteen. (That's when I started bleaching it—the thinking being that if it's bright yellow, it's *invisible.*)

The segment producer came into my dressing room to prepare me for the show. The typical format of *Politically Incorrect* involves discussion about topics in the news that day, ranging from politics to pop culture. But this show, I was told, would be almost entirely about us—Guy and me. My plan was to keep it light and jokey, but also sincere.

The producer said Bill would ask me to repeat the joke in question.

"No! Really? It will die like that! Can't you play the clip from *Conan?*"

"No. We can't get the rights."

NBC had vowed never to rebroadcast the joke in any form, including clips. The only topic of tonight's show was that joke, and there was no clip available. I would have to repeat the joke; it was the only way. Great.

Before the producer left the room, she mentioned her annoyance over Guy Aoki's request for extra seats in the audience.

"Really?" I asked. "How many people does he have out there?"

"Sixty."

"Sixteen??? He has sixteen people in the audience?? Are you fucking serious? I'm dead."

She had to work up the gumption to tell me I had misheard her. Then she rallied:

"Um, SixTEE."

That motherfucker had sixty pissed-off people in the audience, and all I had were two professional stoner-comedians in the *green-room*. I had one more question:

"How many seats are there in the audience *all together*?"

"One hundred and twenty-five."

Kill me. Please. Please take my life.

As it happened, there was no way to stop time, and before I knew it, *this* was happening:

Bill Maher introduced Guy Aoki, me, David Spade, and an actress named Anne-Marie Johnson, most famous for being on the spin-off of *What's Happening!!* called *What's Happening Now!* Right off the bat, Bill asked me to repeat the joke. I did my best, but I was pretty mojo-less. The punch line was met with boos—sixty of them, as promised—which sent me spiraling downward and into a sinkhole of incoherence.

Here's a partial transcript I found on Guy Aoki's Wikipedia page that pretty much says it all. (Feel free to wince at my enlistment of the word "dude.")

MAHER: *Wait a minute. So you're telling me—so you are telling me, sir, that there is some joke that could use the word "chink" done correctly, satirically, that would be okay.*

AOKI: *I think it would definitely be okay.*

MAHER: *Wait a second, that's what you said. You said, "It just wasn't done correctly." So what—give me an example—*

AOKI: *No, I am just addressing one of the points she said, which was satire. I'm saying it wasn't good satire, anyway.*

SILVERMAN: *That's objective, dude.*

MAHER: *That's implying that some joke would be of such good satire that she could have said "chink."*

AOKI: *What she could have said—what she could have said? She could have said, "I hate Chinese people. I love Chinese people." Would have gone, "Okay, funny joke, ha-ha." And that would have been over with.*

SILVERMAN: *That's not the point of the joke. The joke is making fun—*

ANNE-MARIE JOHNSON: *That's the question. Where is the joke?*

[*Applause.*]

AOKI: *The point is you used a slur that you thought you could get away with on national television.*

SILVERMAN: *That's true. Racism is so—exists, you know, and it's not gonna go away.*

AOKI: *It does?*

SILVERMAN: *It's not gonna go away through censorship. Especially censorship with comics.*

AOKI: *So we should just keep bad jokes and offend people over and over again.*

SILVERMAN: *You're a douchebag, man.*

AOKI: [*with mock surprise*]: *Oh oh! Oh oh!*

Bill was pretty spectacular in his defense of me and, more important, in defense of comedy, subjectivity, and free speech. Spade was hilarious as my no-help-whatsoever friend on the panel. He said practically nothing until the third or fourth segment, when he eked out something like "How come there aren't any white people parades?" Thanks, David. Anne-Marie was a typical C-list actress who was superpsyched to be on *Politically Incorrect* and show the world how smart she wasn't.

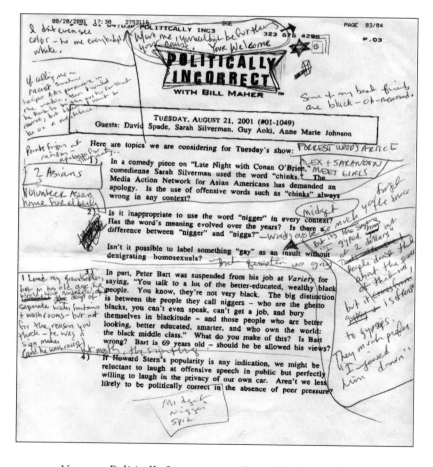

Notes on a Politically Incorrect *prep sheet, which they e-mail out to panelists the night before the show*

(1)

(A) The joke points a ~~finger~~ at racism just like its your job to point a finger at racism. ~~▬▬~~ ~~supposed to apologize for illuminating~~ I don't think its appropriate to ~~do~~ apologize for illuminating racism differently than you. (counterproductive)

(sincerly) ✗ (B) There one only 2 Asian people I know ~~that I did like~~

(C) Volunteer at Asian home for Elderly

(D) Some of my best friends are black. oh. nevermind.

(E) If calling me a racist... somehow furthers the ~~cause of~~ perserverence of Asians. in America.

(F) I didn't even see color...

(G) ~~Alex Brister~~ Susan Smarden — meet girls

Notes on the reverse side of the Politically Incorrect *prep sheet*

I think there is a need for cultural checks and balances, and I believe Guy Aoki has an important job. I just think he's shitty at it. His campaign against me mostly served to raise my profile as a comedian, and to make him look whiny, weak, and, worst of all, dense. I sympathize, because the job of fighting to change broad cultural attitudes is really hard, and I don't pretend to know how to go about it. What I might have suggested is that Guy seek a bigger and better target than me—a not-very-well-known comic who made a joke about racism on a late-night talk show, a joke that he misinterpreted. He might have found a meatier dish in, say, the show *Chicago Hope*. I'm not saying I had a problem with it personally, but that show did take place in a medical center based on Northwestern Memorial—a real Chicago hospital with a high percentage of Asian doctors, while the TV version featured exactly none (a fact I learned from Forrest G. Wood, a white man who wrote an article called "Hollywood and the Asian Exclusion"). Guy could have dined out on that for a year.

Guy Aoki: Heart in Right Place, Head Up Wrong Place

Guy would have really thrived in the 1930s, '40s, and '50s. A man like him, with moderate intelligence, and maybe a good helping of courage and tenacity, could have made a name for himself by attacking the networks and studios who delivered Stepin Fetchit, Amos and Andy, and Al Jolson to American audiences. But in recent decades, an effective cultural crusader requires a more nuanced perception of irony and context.

I grew up watching Archie Bunker, the ignorant racist character created by Norman Lear, who was, himself, famously devoted to advancing racial tolerance and progressive cultural values. Archie Bunker's racism was Lear's vessel for delivering comedy with a social message. Had Guy Aoki been operating in the '70s, he might have attacked Norman Lear as a racist. The bad news for guys like Aoki is that, not only are the progressive messages out there today more refined and sense-of-irony dependent, but racist messages are more oblique, too. Right-wing Americans who appear in mainstream media are not out there calling black people "niggers," or saying "The Klan has good ideas." Instead, they're questioning the legitimacy of Obama's presidency by accusing him of being born in Africa, or of being a Muslim. Or they're having "tea parties," and calling Obama a "communist" and a "Nazi." The entire Fox News Channel is a twenty-four-hour-a-day racism engine, but it's all coded, all implied. Lou Dobbs used to scream on CNN about "immigration," not "filthy Mexicans." I suspect the racist messages about Asians that permeate the media are even subtler, and therefore more difficult to combat.

Why It Is a Mistake to Deconstruct One's Self

As much as my dustup with Guy Aoki was about current cultural trends, it was, of course, also about me, and my choices as a comedian.

In general, I never want to deconstruct what I do because I worry it can be identity crisis-y. There is this thing in physics called the observer effect, which basically says that you can never purely observe anything because the presence of the observer changes the thing. That's my fear about deconstructing comedy. Say someone says to you, "I love how when you smile you do that thing with your lip." And you think, *What thing with my lip??* And for the rest of your fucking life you are too self-conscious to really truly organically smile. It's been tainted. Becoming too self-aware, too cognizant of your own process.

A brief digression: A lot of comics think the real threat of mental blockage lies in becoming *happy.* They fear that happiness or even just dealing with their shit might make them not funny anymore. To me, that's a bunch of romanticized bullshit. I don't know. I guess if you write your best stuff when you're miserable, maybe, but I don't. I'm paralyzed when I'm miserable. I sleep. A lot. I will always try to be happy. I don't think people really understand the value of happiness until they know what it's like to be in that very, very dark place. It's not romantic. Not even a little.

I Will Now Deconstruct Myself

When I was nineteen my stand-up was about the newest and most important things in my life: sex and drugs. My roommates and I had painted our apartment the exact shade of purple to match our twelve-dollar bong.

I was earnest and sensitive and, believe it or not, politically correct to the max. Example: My friend Mark Cohen—every comic's favorite comic and the quickest mind anyone knew—grabbed a nickel from our table at the Washington Square Diner, stuck it on his forehead, and yelped, "Jewish Ash Wednesday!"

Everyone laughed but me. I was upset. Cohen (Coco) rolled his eyes at me for ruining his fun, but I couldn't help it. I was hurt that he would perpetuate a stereotype like that.

I know.

① Jimmy Kimmel, Everyone—
He's fat and has no
charisma.
you better
(Watch your back, Danny
Aiello!)

? Danny — how did Delaventura get
cancelled?? You have everything America
wants in a leading man — YOUR FAT, OLD UGLY

Index card for my first joke after Jimmy Kimmel introduced me at the Hugh Hefner roast. It was the first time I remember meeting Jimmy (though he says we met once before).

The truth is, from that time up to now, *inside,* I haven't changed. My outer shell may mutate, I may come to embrace the things that scare and upset me, but it all comes from the same *place.* At some point, I figured that it would be more effective and far funnier to embrace the ugliest, most terrifying things in the world—the Holocaust, racism, rape, et cetera. But for the sake of comedy, and the comedian's personal sanity, this requires a certain emotional distance. It's akin to being a shrink or a social worker. You might think that the most sensitive, empathetic person would make the best social worker, but that person would end up being soup on the floor. It really takes someone strong—someone, dare I say, with a big fat wall up—to work in a pool of heartbreak all day and not want to fucking kill yourself. But adopting a persona at once ignorant and arrogant allowed me to say what I didn't mean, even preach the opposite of what I believed. For me, it was a funny way to be sincere. And like the jokes in a roast, the hope is that the genuine sentiment—maybe even a *goodness* underneath the joke (however brutal) transcends. The problem with this formula is that once the irony becomes the audience's *expectation*, the surprise is gone.

I Get Tricked into Being a Dick

With all the religious and racial material I've done, the bulk of complaints and outcry have come from the advocates of what must be the hardest suffering of all minorities: über-rich, thin, young blondes.

In June of 2007, I was hired to host the *MTV Movie Awards*. As part of my standard hosting duties, I went onstage at the top of the show and told jokes about celebrities and current events in pop culture. In general, I don't do those kinds of jokes in my regular stand-up. The only time I really do that is when it's required, like at a roast (and that is done with love), or at events like the *Movie Awards*.

One of the biggest events in pop culture at that time was the impending lockup of Paris Hilton. To refresh your memory, Paris was sentenced to a brief stay at the L.A. county jail for drunk driving, then violating her parole and driving drunk again. Here's what I said onstage about her (a great joke written by Jonathan Kimmel, with a tagline by me):

In a couple of days, Paris Hilton is going to jail. The judge says that it's gonna be a no-frills thing, and that is ridiculous. As a matter of fact, I hear that in order to make her feel more comfortable in prison, the guards are gonna paint the bars to look like penises. I just worry that she's gonna break her teeth on those things.

What can't be conveyed in the above quote is the audience's reaction. When I said, "Paris Hilton is going to jail," the crowd erupted into a sustained, almost primal frenzy of cheers and applause. Not even the announcement of free universal health care could have incited such passion. The camera trained on her coupled with the eruption of cheers at her impending imprisonment made my heart sink. This was not a jibe at the roast of an old salt. She was a Christian thrown to the lions in an arena of Romans cheering her imminent demise.

I had no moral qualms, in theory, with joking about Paris's incarceration—it's what late-night talk-show hosts had been doing for weeks. But to set her up to be jeered to her face by thousands on live television during the most vulnerable, frightening moment of her life—needless to say, that took the fun out of the "all in good fun" essence I intended. Whether it was an innocent oversight, or a very calculating one, no one producing the show informed me until minutes before I went onstage that Paris would be in the audience. With that very late piece of information, I didn't stop to concentrate, to seriously imagine how that whole moment might come together.

The next morning I Googled myself and discovered that my joke had set the Internet ablaze. The *L.A. Times* described my joke as "a cruel beat-down on Hilton." Even on my own unofficial Web site, one visitor—and presumably a fan—posted: "That was one of the meanest things I have ever witnessed." Everywhere I looked, I saw words like "cruel," "mean," "vicious," and "nasty." Web sites and blogs were consumed with the question of whether or not I had gone too far, of whether or not I was a bitch. Paris weighed in with an unequivocal yes. If Guy Aoki had stirred up just a fraction of this level of outrage with my "Chink" joke, he would still be jacking off to it now.

In fact, I felt much worse about this than I did about upsetting Aoki. He'd misunderstood a joke. Paris was genuinely a *victim* of a joke. I felt horribly guilty. At the time, I was writing the second season of *The Sarah Silverman Program*, but I was so disturbed that I could not focus on work. I left the writers' room and wrote a letter to Paris, who was now, on top of being hurt, in jail.

It was surely one of the least important media controversies in history. And I was probably the only person specifically Googling the story, so most of it was probably just playing out in the space between my laptop and my eyeballs. But what I took away from it all was, if I ever did another MTV awards show, I needed to be more careful about the jokes I told.

I Do Another MTV Awards Show, and Am Not Careful About the Jokes I Tell

---

Several months later, when MTV asked me to do a couple of minutes of stand-up at the *Video Music Awards*, it sounded like fun. I guess MTV awards shows are like childbirth: God makes you forget the pain so that you'll do it again, which makes sense, as MTV awards shows are crucial to the survival of the human species.

I had a week to put some jokes together, not realizing that I would be perceived, essentially, as hosting the show. That's what an awards show host on MTV does—a few minutes at the top, after the opening number.

In this case, the opening number was Britney Spears. Britney was not performing merely to support the network that made her famous, but to launch a comeback—from musical oblivion, pregnancy pudge, and willful baldness. Anytime you do stand-up on a show like this, you have to do a couple jokes on the performance you just followed as a segue into the bulk of your act. Since I followed Britney, I had to do a couple of jokes on her before I moved on. But you have to understand that there was no doubt in my mind that she would be amazing. Her brilliance has always been in blowing the lid off the live *MTV Video Music Awards*: the Catholic schoolgirl, the Madonna kiss, the boa constrictor. She is MTV's homerun queen.

Unfortunately for both of us, Britney's performance was a complete abortion. I don't mean that snarkily—I just state it as scientific fact. She looked in turns tentative, nervous, and listless; her lip-synching was distractingly bad, and though her body was still outstanding by almost any standard, it fell short of what the public had come to expect from her, and was exposed for the world's scrutiny by an unforgiving sequined bikini.

But I would only learn how catastrophic her performance was much later in the night. People think that comics sit casually watching a show, then waltz onto the stage and talk off the top of their heads. The truth is that I was crafting specific jokes all week, and during Britney's live performance, I wasn't watching her, I was pacing manically, going over my material.

Immediately after Britney wrapped up her train wreck and scurried off the stage in disgrace, I marched out there, clueless, and said this:

Britney Spears, everyone. Wow. She is amazing. I mean she's twenty-five years old, and she's already accomplished everything she's going to accomplish in her life. It's mind-blowing. And she's so grown up. She's a mother. It's crazy. It's weird to think that just a few years ago on this very show she was this, like, sweet innocent little girl in slutty clothes writhing around with a python . . . But have you seen Britney's kids? Oh my god, they are the most adorable mistakes you will ever see. They are as cute as the hairless vagina they came out of . . .

It must have seemed akin to making jokes about a hit-and-run victim as they were getting loaded into an ambulance. But I'm telling you, I had no idea there'd been an accident.

After the obligatory Britney portion of my monologue, I segued to other jokes I was more excited about. My appearance seemed to go well, and the rest of the night was a blast. When I woke up the next morning, I went online to find that my performance was eviscerated.

The media-Internet outrage was way more intense than it had been after the Paris Hilton debacle. Paris was a divisive figure, and many people took delight in her comeuppance. But Britney had become this tragic figure, and evidently I had kicked her when she was down. The fact that I'd made jokes about her children (though if you look at the text, you'll notice it was about *her*, not anything specific about her children) was widely viewed as hitting below the belt. Bloggers seized the opportunity to attack me—my looks, my lack of talent, my heartlessness. The only thing they were more brutal toward was Britney's extra eight pounds.

To make matters far worse, Britney's representatives lied to the press. They contended that I was the *cause* of Britney's disastrous performance. According to them, she had seen my jokes at rehearsal and was so devastated that she was unable to regain her composure by the time she got onstage. The proof that this was false lies in MTV's evil genius. MTV's producers very deliberately instructed me *NOT* to recite my actual jokes in rehearsal. Dress rehearsal is more for the nailing down of lighting and music cues. Instead, I walked out on stage and said, "Joke, joke, joke, blah, blah blah, enjoy the show." Wisely, they didn't want to be held responsible for anything I said on live TV. But they always want the benefits of any controversy or embarrassment that happens on their airwaves. I loved that they didn't want to know the jokes I was doing because it gave me total freedom in a world normally straightjacketed by the network's Standards and Practices Department. (MTV presents itself as the ultimate destination for hip and edgy, but from a corporate perspective, it's a children's network, closely monitored by parents and advertisers.) I was annoyed that the network had no problem hanging me out to dry. Is that what I did to Britney or Paris?

Regardless of the Spears camp's lies, and of MTV's having totally set me up for this, I had no interest in drama or feuds with girls two-thirds my age. I sat back down at my old apology-writing desk, its seat still warm from earlier in the summer, and sent Britney a letter, expressing what was my sincere regret. I don't know if she received it.

I'm a comic known for dirty jokes, Britney is a singer of frothy pop songs, and the *VMA* is an award show for the dying art of music videos, which airs on a channel that barely shows them anymore. In other words, this controversy was equally as unimportant in the world—if not more so—as the Paris Hilton incident. But I can't help noticing that the public outrage was far greater in both instances than it was over my alleged offense against the Asian American community. A wider swath of Americans expressed their condemnation of me in the Britney and Paris melees.

Maybe it's that people view Asian Americans, a population known for high levels of college enrollment and enormous success in small business, as a people who can take care of themselves and don't need defending, whereas, thin, white, young blond women are enjoyable to have sex with. It makes perfect sense. They're as much a sacred symbol of America as the bald eagle and the Humvee. I had basically taken a shit on the head of a bald eagle. Is it possible that what truly caused me to do it was the deep-seated anger and resentment of a dark, hairy, backwoods Jew toward these dainty, fair-haired embodiments of American perfection?

Nah. But I knew you were thinking that, so I felt a need to say it first.

*   *   *

To all you sensitive sallys out there who spend your time scribing angry letters, I have great news: Scientific models show that, in the not-too-distant future, all the races will become so completely interbred that humanity will have a monolithic caramelish color and common facial features. There won't be blonds or hairy Jews anymore. Words like "Chink" will cease to have meaning. They will be relics, along with those who use them for comedy. Which is exactly why I am past that meta-racist shit and onto poop and pee. Onward and downward!

CALLS FROM SCHLEPPY

Dad (in front of an old pic of himself) at his surprise seventieth birthday party in New Hampshire

Since the day I moved away from home my dad has called me every Saturday. I learned fairly early not to pick up when I saw it was him, as more often than not, at least to me, his messages were comedy gold and I wanted them on tape. My dad is a weirdo. Most all of his friends in New Hampshire are literally from summer camp. They continue to call him by his childhood nickname—Schleppy. When he and my stepmother, Janice, go to Boca Raton for the winter, my father sits at Starbucks and heckles rich people as they walk in and out, saying things like, "Hey, nice Mercedes! That could probably feed eighty thousand people in India, but, no, you need it. Good job!" He has been punched in the face three winters in a row.

The following are a few voice-mails from my father, transcribed by me. I wrote it, as best I could, phonetically—to account for his very thick New England accent, as I feel it adds an important layer of understanding. You may pick up on his carefree sense of humor, his penchant for dialing the wrong number, and his vocal dislike of rich people. Here are a few samplings for your enjoyment.

6/13/09, 11:10 A.M.

Dad: Hey, Baby! Guess who? It's You-ah daddy! Happy Shubbus. I say that 'cause you-ah friend, Jeffrey Ross, is in Israel. And I've been spending time with you'ah nieces. I took Shi Shi [*my niece Ashira*] to Chuckie Cheese twice—she is SO FUCKIN' CUTE. Gimme a call when ya get a chance, um, I leave in a coupla ow-ahs but I'll be in my caah for an ow-ah oah two—know whe-ah I'm goin'? I am goin' to . . . my fiftieth fuckin' reuinion of UNH! It took fifty fuckin' yee-ahs to get hee-ah. Goin' through it, it was all those days with you and Laura and Jodyne and Susie and aggravation and business and blah blah blah. And you look back on it, and it seemed like it took twenty minutes—the whole god-damn thing! It's amazin'. It took so long to get here, just to look back so quickly. So watch out, 'cause you-ah only goin' one way, and that's oldah! And once you can no longah doin' sumthin', that's forevah. I been pretty goddamn lucky so fah. I love you. That's my homily fo-ah the day. I love you. Give me a call if you get a chance, like if you-ah walkin' you-ah dog o'ah sumthin' boring like that. And I'll talk to ya latah. MMMMMUAHHH. [*Then, to himself*] Uh . . . shut off phone.

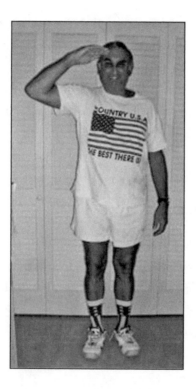

Dad's annual Fourth of July uniform

03/28/09, 1:49 P.M.

Hello, Sarah! It's you-ah daddy, callin' from Boca Raton, Flarida, whey-ah they-ah ah a lot of entitled people. They whey-ah expensive watches that tell time just like my Timex, and they drive very expensive cahhs that help people to know how rich they ahh, and that they ah entitled so if you see one of them, you'll know to act prop-ah-ly. I love you and I will talk to you again soon. Bye-bye.

03/14/09, 11:54 A.M.

Oh shit I dialed the wrong numbah. He hee. That's a good one. Hi, Honey, you wah wondahful last night [*I was on* Real Time with Bill Maher], really, I gutta watch it again . . . Arhh! I'm yawnin' 'cause I just woke up from a little nappy cause I'm tryin' to get a little sleep he-yah 'cause I'm goin' to a BIG wedding tonight with big rich people who I don't even know. Jesus Christ, it's like they all like you-ah evil step-muthah so much they invite us to these goddamn weddings. Oh well. Luckily I gut a tuxedo that I bought at Good Will—did you know that? Did you know that I bought it at the Jewish Good Will store—a goah-juss tuxedo fo-ah thirty-seven dollahs and fifty cents on sale, half price, it was originally seventy-five dollahs, and it is goah-juss. I LOVE telling people how much I paid far it. [*Big loud yawn.*] I need a little bit mo-ah nap. Alright, Honey, I love you. Gimme a call when ya get a chance. Talk to ya latah. Bye-bye.

3/07/09, 10:40 A.M.

Excuse me but, who is this? Is it really you? [*Sing-songy.*] Maybe it is and maybe it isn't.

How ya doin', Sweetie? Ahhhhhh, gimme a call when you getta chance. I'm on my way to the beach club far an ol' swimaroony, you wanna come with me? [*I'm in L.A. and he's in Florida.*] Rich people live at the beach club, po-ah people have to drive they'ah.

[*Sing-songy again.*] Love you. Talk to you laterrrr. [← *The hard "r" is his way of making fun of how I talk.*] Bye-bye, Dahlin'. Mmuah.

2/28/09, 2:01 P.M.

DAD: A hundred bottles of bee-ah on the wall, a hundred bottles of bee-ah, take one down, drink it down, ninety-nine bottles of bee-ah on the wall. Ninety-nine bottles of bee-ah on the wall, ninety-nine bottles of bee-ah, take one down—whoop

JANICE [*his wife, in the background*]: Hi, Sarah! Donald, stop it.

DAD: I only had ninety-eight mo-ah to go—

JANICE: Call us when you wake up in the mo-ahning 'cause we-ah going out in about fifty-five minutes—

DAD [*to Janice*]: Yeah, you tell ha that you know what she does, Janice?

JANICE: What?

DAD: She calls knowin' we-ah not hee-ah so she can leave a fuckin' message.

JANICE: Call us when you wake up, Sweetie.

DAD: Oh shit . . . [*I'm guessing he spilled something.*]

JANICE: Love you.

DAD: Love you, bye, Honey.

2/7/09, 11:48 A.M.

That's so weird! 'Cause I thought I was callin' Laura, and I called Sarah! I don't mind callin' Sarah. It was on my list of things to do anyway. Call me back when you get a chance. Don't try and pull the old bullshit of callin' me tonight when you know I'm out. I don't fall for that one anymo-ah. Evah since it happened forty weeks in a row. All right, Honey. I love you. Give me a call. Bye, Sweetie.

1/29/09, 1:17 P.M.

Jesus, Sarah! I was callin' Mark Reingold! But I was pretty surprised when you answered the phone with you-ah answerin' machine. I guess I pressed the wrong button on the phone. Just remember this: I'm pretty fuckin' old and things like that can happen. I just made a quick turn. I'm drivin'. Talkin' to you on Bluetooth. Um, all right, Sweethawt. I love you, bye . . . [*Several beats.*] How do I shut this thing off?

Dad was so excited to visit the set of my show that he fell asleep within, oh, I'd say, twelve minutes.

1/23/09, 9:01 A.M.

[Sung to a made-up tune, while visiting the three L.A. daughters—Laura, Jodyne, and me. He insists on staying at a Ramada Inn nearby because there's a Starbucks in it.]

This is you-ah daddy. It's really, really me.
I'm callin' to tell you some oppahtunity.
The first choice is, to not meet us. The second choice is to go
    for a walk with Janny.
The third choice is to meet me at Stahbucks fahr a coffee.
The fou-ath choice is a quick Stahbucks coffee
. . . and a walk with Janice.
Those ah you-ah choices; I hope they satisfy you.
If they don't, then you'ah a dirty Jewwww.

[Spoken] Love you. Bye-bye.

9/14/08, 9:29 A.M.

[Note: New Hampshire still has the kind of car wash where you turn off your car, put it in neutral, and ride through.]

Hey, Baby, guess who? It's you-ah daddy! Guess whey-ah I am? The cah wash! Janice is at a baby showah and—oy. Oy! Jesus fuckin' Christ. My fuckin' windows ah down and the button to put 'em up won't work and I'm gettin' fuckin' soaked. [Several beats.] The whole cah is soaked. Oy. [Then] Okay, love you, Dahlin'.

1/17/09, 9:10 A.M.

I remembah when you whuh a tiny baby and I had to lift those tiny legs and wipe the SHIT out of you-ah tuchus. It was fuckin' disgustin'. All right. If you get a chance—I know you-ah really busy—give a call back to the guy who gave you life. Love you. Bye.

THE MOST IMPORTANT THING IN LIFE: BEING ON TV

Pussyface

Dave Rath is a friend to all comics. He's a manager, but he's funny and silly and considered one of us. Whenever I would visit L.A., I stayed with Dave. He lived in a big house with a bunch of comics—

Todd Glass, Brian Posehn, and Alan Murray. Dave is like a brother to me, and the deal was that if he didn't get lucky that night I could sleep in his big bed with him; if he did, I was on the couch.

I slept in his bed one night and, in a bout of what I can only guess was nocturnal nostalgia, I wet the bed. I woke up early in the morning, and realizing what had happened, I knew I had to say something right away.

"Dave," I nudged him awake. "Dave, I peed in your bed, I'm sorry!" Dave didn't move. Didn't even open his eyes. Just murmured through his sleepy lips,

"It's okay, just put a towel down and go back to sleep."

Friends for life.

During one L.A. visit, I had to go straight to the Laugh Factory from the airport for a show before I could get to Rath's and settle in. I called him and told him to meet me at the club, which was just yards down the hill from where he lived.

I arrived at the Laugh Factory, put my luggage in the ticket booth, and sat in the back of the room, arranging my notes and figuring out my set. I looked up and there was Rath. I jumped to my feet and gave him a hug and a friendly kiss on the lips. As we pulled back, I noticed that his goatee left an imprint on my face. A viscous, slimy goatee of my own. Bracing for what I already knew in my heart to be true, I whispered through pained horror, "Were you just eating pussy?" His eyes popped open as if a magician just guessed his card.

"Oh my god! Yes!"

"Wash your face!" I gagged, running to the ladies' room to wash my own, slippery, *strange-lady's-vagina-on-my-face* face. Mortified, Dave followed suit.

To recap: I urinated on Dave's legs, and he got vagina juice on my face. Taken separately, these acts might seem highly regrettable, but I like to think this exchange of fluids functioned as a kind of "friendship sealant." A really fucking gross friendship sealant.

Garry Shandling Is More Like the Buddha Than One Might Have Guessed (Though I Say This Never Having Met the Buddha Personally . . .)

Dave was part of a regular Sunday-afternoon basketball game at Garry Shandling's house, and on one afternoon in 1995 he brought me along. I was such a huge fan of Garry's and was completely in awe; it's difficult to meet your idols. Not, I suppose, as difficult as living in a refugee camp in the Sudan, on the brink of starvation and murder, but I did find myself pretty tongue-tied. Still, I was able to show some prowess on the court, and I piqued Garry's interest enough that he came to see me do stand-up. About a year or so later, he and writer Alan Zweibel created a role for me on an episode of *The Larry Sanders Show* as one of the writers on the show-within-the-show. It was probably my biggest career thrill since getting hired to be an actual writer at *Saturday Night Live*. There was just one thing standing between me and a whole new level of career prestige: my agent.

I got a call from Justin, the writers' assistant at *Sanders*, whom I knew from basketball at Garry's house. He said, "You should know this. I was asked to call your agent at CAA to get tape on you, so that the other writers here could get familiar with you and write the part in your voice. But when I made the request for your tape, your agent said, "Well, what's the part, because I've got lots of girls?"

"What?"

I was baffled.

"Your agent tried to pitch other actresses for a role that is being written for you."

By this point I was no stranger to show-biz disenchantment, but still, I mean, really? I confronted my agent about it, and he took me to lunch to smooth it over. He showed up with a bunch of movie scripts for me to read. That was the "good guy" part of his strategy. He also had a "bad guy" component, which consisted of belittling me with comments like, "Well, you're not hot," and, "You're a hard sell—why would anyone want to cast you when they could get X or Y?"

When we left the restaurant, in what could have only been genius foresight on his part to make this story fucking perfect, he realized he had no cash and asked me for money for the valet. I gave him enough for the fee and a tip—but he gave me the extra money back saying, "Don't tip, it's figured into the fee." Some people just never disappoint. I waited for him to leave and gave the valet his tip along with mine. After this most disheartening afternoon, I called my manager and told him I wanted to fire CAA, but the diabolical bastards went ahead and dropped me first. They really must be good at what they do, though, because ten years later, they signed me again, and I'm still with them.

Despite all the above, I did end up doing the part on *Sanders*, appearing in three episodes. Getting to work on one of my all-time-favorite comedies was not only a life highlight but also a tremendous learning experience. The show was brilliantly written, of course, but now I could see that it was just as brilliantly *run*. Garry would encourage the actors to go off the page at any impulse. This was something I hadn't encountered before. And I saw that a writer not married to his own words is a winning combination. Garry would say, "Just say what the line means, and don't worry about the words. If you can convey it by just saying 'pineapple' so be it." It was fun and it was loose.

When people tried to capture the magic of *Sanders* in subsequent imitations, they stole the wrong thing. They made all these copycat shows that took place behind the scenes of some kind of television program. But the brilliance of *Sanders* wasn't its setting, but its *process*. They would have had to steal *Garry himself*.

I gleaned so much from Garry I don't know how I can ever repay him. From his stand-up I learned to embrace the quiet moments, rather than to fear them. And he taught me that while some things come too early, nothing comes too late. I thank God that I didn't get the role in *Suddenly Susan* that I auditioned for, and that I got fired from the pilot of an NBC sitcom called *Pride and Joy*, in which I was to play a wife, career woman, and mother with two wacky neighbors. I'm grateful that I had my time on *SNL*, and I'm grateful that it was short—it didn't wind up defining me. Garry helped me realize that fifteen years was not too long to be in this business before getting a chance at a show of my own. And he gave me an invaluable warning: Nobody in show business will ever tell you that you're taking on too much. No agent, executive, or producer will ever say, "Sarah, you're working too many weeks in a row for your own good," or "You're doing too many episodes and their quality might be sacrificed." Garry emphasized that it would be up to me to set limits, to know what I can and cannot do, and that "quality of life" does not mean "the most money you can possibly make."

So, thank you, Garry Emmanuel Shandling, for being my teacher and my friend. I write this because, realistically, it is very likely I may not get the chance to say it on stage at an awards show. Although that dream might not come true, I'm still holding out hope that I will someday get my face on money. (Please, no pesos.)

To Not Be Suze

When a female comic is cast in a film role, her character tends to be one of the following: the bitchy ex-wife; the lead character's cunty girlfriend before he finds out what love can *really* be; or the quirky best friend, a character who exists purely to convey to the audience information about the main protagonist ("but you're a lawyer and he loves you!"). She may also play the female lead in a comedy serving her male counterpart thusly: "You're acting like a child! When are you gonna get your shit together and get a job?"

I'm not unproud to say that I've played all of these. And, not to brag, but as I write these very words, a stack of scripts sits just inches away from me, all with roles like the above. And they are all named "Suze." If not literally, then most definitely in essence. In homes all around my neighborhood, there are more such screenplays being generated, all equipped with two-dimensional Suzes whose sole purpose is to facilitate more complex three-dimensional roles.

But I'm lucky, I can always sustain myself with stand-up, which I love. Because of stand-up one renegade producer with genius instincts and balls of steel took a chance and gave me a leading role in a film that would define a generation and redeem the world. The film was called *Sarah Silverman: Jesus Is Magic*, and that producer was me. I didn't even have to blow me to get the job, but I did anyway.

An early set list for Jesus Is Magic

Jesus Is Magic combined concert footage of my stand-up with music videos of my songs and scripted scenes. Soon after its run, Comedy Central approached me about doing a show. They offered me total creative freedom. Anything I wanted. Plus, there was the prestige of being on a network that has comedy right in its name! Fancy! The amazingly talented writing team of Rob Schrab and Dan Harmon came aboard to collaborate with me on creating a pilot (more about them later). After fourteen years in the business I finally had the chance to write my dream part and show the world what I was *really* capable of. And when we were done writing, shooting, and editing the pilot, my boyfriend and I sat down to watch it.

He pointed out that in the first five minutes, my character ignored dying children on her television screen, lied to get out of helping a friend move, and threw a tantrum when a walkathon for the handicapped blocked off access to a convenience store. In short, he said, I seemed to be playing a cunt.

"How about that," I thought aloud.

But it wasn't the same thing at all. My character on *The Sarah Silverman Program* is three dimensional, with layers and back story, and big love in her heart. I would argue that she's less a cunt than a clueless, arrogant ignoramus in search of an identity. She doesn't exist merely as a vessel to deliver exposition. And her name is not "Suze."

Mein Kampf: Preface

Anyone who works at Comedy Central and reads this will probably appreciate when I say that I am *fully* aware that I can be a gigantic pain in the ass. I don't say this proudly, only as fact, and I imagine that if I hadn't been a pain in their ass, my show might have been a very different one. I'm only guessing that what follows will be interesting to you, dear reader, because it's way interesting to me. So with no further adoooo, here are some of our more notable, funny, and/or retarded behind-the-scenes struggles.

Rob, me, Steve, and Brian taking a break outside Stage 5

Mein Kampf, Part One: Steve

I knew right away that I wanted my buddy Steve Agee in the show. I met him in the late nineties when he was a guitarist in a play that another friend, Dave Juskow, had written and performed at a small theater in Hollywood. Steve and I talked after the show and immediately connected over our mutual struggles with depression. We became fast friends, and before long we were spending every night at my apartment, smoking weed, playing Nintendo 64 (*GoldenEye* and *007* in particular) and *You Don't Know Jack* (TV and movie versions), and making each other laugh to the point of tears.

Steve's real passion lies in making elaborate home videos, starring himself. My personal favorites are an ongoing holiday series. On

Thanksgiving, Christmas, Halloween, etc., he films himself lying naked in bed, vigorously masturbating with a black rectangle censoring his penis—while moaning in ecstasy about various things associated with each particular holiday: "Ooohhh cranberry sauce. Oh yeah, stuffing. Ohhhh family arguments, oh god fucking yams . . ." For me, this was more than enough evidence that Steve was ready to star in a television series.

Steve Agee pretends to smoke.

When it came time to cast *TSSP*, Rob, Dan, and I told Comedy Central we wanted Steve. We had, after all, already written the part of "Steve" for Steve. But since they hadn't heard of him, much less seen him act, and he had literally no résumé, they were concerned about giving him a lead role in a series. So we had Steve send them his home movies. Incomprehensibly, holiday-themed masturbating still did not convince the network that Steve could handle this or any job. We had to fight them, but we were ready to die on that hill—and they knew it. Incidentally, Steve, if you're reading this, you're welcome. Hope you've enjoyed all the pussy.

Mein Kampf, Part Two: Rob Schrab Rapes Fruit

Rob Schrab is the hilarious, creepy, gorgeous, tortured, sweet, gentle, slender man who co-created *TSSP* along with his partner, Dan Harmon, and me. Rob is an executive producer, one of the lead writers, and the main director, as well as a recurring cast member playing multiple roles. His previous project with Harmon had been a pilot for Fox called "Heat Vision and Jack," starring Jack Black and directed by Ben Stiller. It's legendary for being one of the funniest pilots that never got picked up, courtesy of Fox. Rob and Dan then created Channel 101, one of the very first Web sites devoted to short comedy videos and the launching pad for the careers of countless comedic actors, writers, directors, and animators. Dan Harmon is an amazingly talented writer with a unique gift for phrase making, which he demonstrates in lines such as, "I've seen things that would make you crap a book on how to puke," and "I don't know who put a nickel in you, but it's time to make change." After the pilot, however, in an attempt for him and me to not kill each other, Dan left the show and eventually created NBC's hit *Community*.

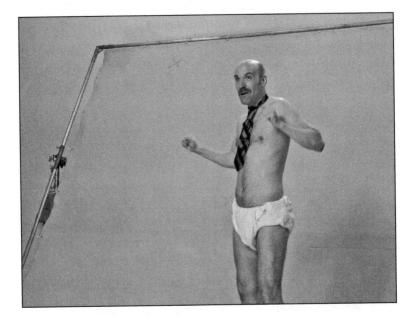

Rob Schrab shooting a fake commercial for TSSP *as "Baby Man Sr."*

We all assumed that Rob would direct the pilot. He'd directed a music video for Deathcab for Cutie, plus countless short films—animated and live action—and had a very distinct visual style. What he hadn't done was direct an episode of narrative television, and this was a serious obstacle at Comedy Central. I told them how much I wanted Rob, but they just wouldn't approve it; he wasn't experienced enough, they insisted, which translates roughly to, "We don't have the ability to know if his work is good unless a million other people have already said so." I wanted them to see in Rob what I did, so I sent them the video that made me fall in love with him in the first place. Steve had shown it to me on one of our stony

Nintendo nights. It was called *Jaws 4: The Revenge*, featuring Michael Caine—or, rather, featuring an orange with the magic marker face of Michael Caine. The character is voiced by Rob, and though he identifies himself as Michael Caine, he sounds instead like a horrible impression of Bill Cosby. The other central character is Jaws, the shark himself, as played by Rob's penis, decorated with tiny eyes pasted onto the head and a dorsal fin affixed to the shaft. Spoiler alert: Michael Caine ends up getting orally raped by the shark. Reminder: Michael Caine = orange; Jaws = Rob's flaccid penis. I can't tell you how many times I've watched this video without tiring of it. Though I have to say, part of the joy is imagining Rob alone in his apartment, starting and stopping his video camera, while his soggy, sticky orange juice–soaked penis dangles in wait for the next shot.

Stunningly, the video did not end the debate between the network and me. But by now I was starting to learn that not giving in—being a pain in the ass, in other words—is actually a very effective strategy for getting your way. Why didn't I realize this when I was eight??

In later seasons, Rob wanted to hire various friends to come aboard as guest directors, and Comedy Central was, again, very reluctant to go with anyone "unproven." Even though they loved how their gamble on Rob turned out. Their lack of trust infuriated Rob, and after one conference call with the network about the issue, he slammed down the phone and shouted, "Why won't they hire this guy?! What had *I* ever done before this show?? I stuck my dick in an orange!!"

Mein Kampf, Part Three: Gigantic, Orange, and Gay

When we finished casting the pilot, we were struck by the fact that Steve Agee and Brian Posehn ("Brian," another main character) are comically similar-looking. They are both extremely tall, large, red-haired, bearded, slovenly, lethargic, nerdy, and bespectacled. To have these two in an ensemble begged for them either to play brothers or lovers. In the main title voice over of the original pilot, we included a joke about not knowing which they were. But as we began to write more scripts, it was clear that the funnier and richer choice was for them to be a couple.

Brian and Steve: America's Sweethearts

Comedy Central was nervous about the idea. Not because of a particular institutional morality—their parent company is MTV Networks, which is pretty gay-friendly—but they had their demographic to consider. The channel's target is basically fourteen-year-old boys and stoners. In theory, at least, it was already a risk to center a show on a female; to then throw gay characters into the mix seemed like too much. The network never said we couldn't do it, but they asked me to reconsider again and again. This was maybe the most offended I've ever been by them. They operate out of fear and second-guessing, I get that, but Jesus, if this network is more worried about the chance that a few date-rapey frat boys might change the channel, then this is not the place for me. Their concern, to me, was so obviously outweighed by the fact that it would not only be hilarious to cast these two gigantic, gentle, stoner slobs as lovers, but it would also be supercool to have gay characters playing against the classic hard-bodied, queeny stereotypes that comprise 99.999 percent of fictionalized homosexual males on TV. The network also seemed either to miss or to diminish the importance of the fact that while Brian's and Steve's characters on the show might be gay, in every other way they act precisely like *fourteen-year-old boys and stoners.* They play video games, eat garbage food, get high, worship heavy metal, and argue over idiotic things. These traits make the gay characters a mirror image of the Comedy Central audience. That, and the fact that they get literally zero pussy.

The network finally backed off because I continued to be stubborn about it, as did Rob Schrab; as did Dan Sterling, the executive producer and head writer. So Comedy Central sucked it up, and with some understandable indigestion over what seemed to them like yet another big gamble, condoned Brian's and Steve's homosexuality.

Brian and Steve became breakout characters pretty much instantly, and the network couldn't get enough of them. Thank God
the show did have two gay main characters, because several years
down the road, a gay cable network would save *The Sarah Silverman
Program* show from ruin. But more on that later.

Mein Kampf, Part Four: Penis, Vagina, God

The Sarah Silverman Program occupies a somewhat tricky piece of territory on Comedy Central. It airs in prime time but, unlike *South
Park,* is not rated TV MA (the most restrictive content rating on
TV). We're rated TV 14 as a result of some sort of network cal-
culus I don't understand. But a lot of what makes the writers and
me laugh is right on the border of being too sexually, scatalogically,
racially, or religiously offensive for the MTV Networks' Standards
and Practices Department. Of course, this is a universal complaint
among all TV comedy writers—everyone wants to do "edgier" material. But the struggle is more intense with us, because doody, farts,
penises, and vaginas are some of the show's main reasons for exist-
ing. Up to this point, anyway, for better or worse, that is just part
of the promise when a show has my name in the title.

Networks tend to be Nurembergian nightmares where the buck
stops nowhere and the right hand never seems to know what the
left hand is doing. The problem in general with the network self-
censorship system is that Standards and Practices are run by human
beings. There is no algorithm for determining what is offensive.
What qualifies as "offensive" is wildly specific to every individual's
weird little brain.

Example #1: In one episode, Steve gets a massage and thinks that the offer of "full release" is an option for him to release his bowels (instead, of course, of the intended liberation of his balls' inner contents). To one of our particular censors, the sound of human feces hitting a massage table was acceptable, but only if that sound suggested that said feces were solid. If the sound suggested too high a liquid content, then we couldn't use it. Their rule of thumb in general is, "Can we defend this to potential complaining viewers or sponsors?" Look, I get it. Loose stools are grosser than solid ones. But the censor is using the context of her own life history with all her hang-ups to answer the question, "Is there a defensible ratio of fiber to water in this stool?"

Example #2: There's essentially no limit to how often we can say "penis," "balls," "scrotum," and "shaft," but female anatomical language is a big, flapping red flag (so to speak). In one episode from the most recent season, our town elects a new mayor. The mayor turns out to be a terrible homophobe and a lunatic who outlaws brunch. She is ultimately exposed to be a lesbian and a secret brunch eater. She attempts to defend herself in this soliloquy:

"Don't listen to her! She doesn't understand what she saw! I don't like brunch or gay sex! [Sighs.] Look, here's what I like, okay? It's this really specific thing. It's not gay. Just listen . . . I like to have a plate of scrambled eggs and onions on my chest, while there's a bushy vagina—mostly covered by panties, but still you can see some hairs escaping—hovering over me. Then I just stuff little chunks of the eggs and onions in my mouth, so I can have the taste of egg and onion, while I look at the bulge of the pubic hairs in the underwear, plus some of the escaping little hairs. Do you know what I mean?"

Standards told us the speech was too graphic, too vivid; "It really takes you right there, visually," they said. It was a long negotiation, but here is the version that was accepted:

> "I like to have a plate of scrambled eggs and onions on my chest, while a woman's genitalia—mostly covered by panties, but not entirely—hovers over me. Then I just stuff little chunks of the eggs and onions in my mouth, so I can have the taste of egg and onion, while I look at the bulge of genitalia in the underwear. Do you know what I mean?"

It was cleansed of nearly all specificity about female anatomy. Their argument was that, in this case, the speech was referring to a sexual fetish, which necessitated less-vivid imagery. Okay. I guess that's understandable. But from another episode in the same cycle is a speech by Laura (my sister on the show and in real life):

> "I found myself interested in some of the video-films specializing in gentlemen using their penises to have anal intercourse with costars of the same gender. After a few hours, I noticed that this act creates an expansion of the man's anal circumference. Much like—have you ever seen Flipper? His blowhole looks like a man's expanded orifice. In the following weeks, I found myself frequently desiring to see the end result of prolonged insertion on a man's 'blowhole.' I guess it's just, well, my cup of tea!"

In the interest of accuracy, this is the *revised* version of her speech. We'd been ordered to remove the words "gaping rectum." But nonetheless, it's WAY more graphic than the previous passage about scrambled eggs and female genitals. In the line below, my character has just been told by Laura that I'd been born with both a penis and a vagina. Devastated and stunned, I ask through tears,

"Were the penis and vagina in separate pieces, or was it like the penis itself was the vagina, but split down the middle with labia?"

According to the censor, "labia," in this instance, was too "graphic," and we were asked to remove it. Labia? Fucking seriously? We can say "penis" and "balls" until the cows come home, but *labia*? I asked our censor if this is what she wanted to teach young girls—that penis is fine and balls are funny but labia—your own body part—is dirty? It was not a stretch to me to view this as telling little girls to be ashamed of their bodies, which genuinely offended me. I expressed these feelings to the censor and prepared to dig in for a long battle. But to my surprise, she saw my point and acknowledged that she had grown up in Catholic schools where female sexual organs were viewed as taboo. I was so impressed by her willingness to admit that her upbringing was clouding her judgment. So congratulations, womankind: Nancy Pelosi is Speaker of the House, and by the time this book is published, "labia" will have been in prime time.

This is the upside of having human beings as censors—some of them, like ours, are reasonable and willing to negotiate. Censors have an important job. You can't have complete lawlessness on a network, and the truth is that restrictions are very often good for creativity. Many times our jokes have been shot down by the censors, forcing us to write better ones. One script called for me to randomly belch the word "rape." S&P would not have it. We fought and fought and just flat-out lost. With no other choice, we pushed ourselves to find another belch-worthy word that would be as inappropriate and nonsensical as "rape." The writers huddled in the conference room with a pot of coffee and unbridled determination, and after several hours, we emerged with a word that not only measured up to "rape," but exceeded it—the perfect combination of phonics and imagery that, when burped, sounded even more re-tarded than our original choice. It was, "Zach Braff," and it was good.

I really respect the ladies (they're all female for some reason) at S&P. To have a job where half your day is spent saying no to—and then being attacked by—arrogant, wise-ass, self-important comedy writers, and to not completely lose your shit, you have to be a tough-skinned motherfucker.

TSSP hasn't incited mass outrage or lost sponsors. As far as I can figure, it has sparked only one controversy: when my character slept with God. For three years, we've pumped violence, farts, doody, genitals, relentless celebration of mind-altering drugs, racial provocation, and Holocaust humor into the basic cable atmosphere. I wore blackface for an entire episode and we never heard a word about it. Only when God (brilliantly played by Tucker Smallwood) was depicted having casual sex did people go apeshit. It's hard to say just exactly what bothered them about it—that God was portrayed as a black man? That he was having a one-night stand? That the one-night stand was a Jew? Or was it that after I had sex with him, I blew him off? Below is just a tiny sampling of the hate mail Comedy Central received after this episode aired:

Message: Sarah Silverman sleeping with God has to be the lowest form of crude humor I have ever heard of. She is talented, but she is deliberately offensive to Religion in general and Christians specifically. Why was it off limits to show Allah on South Park, but ok to show disrespect for God?—you are total hypocrites. I will no longer watch your station—

Message: I look forward to a most wonderful day . . . the day that people like you stand before a holy God and have to answer for this filthy trash. In the meantime, I have permanently blocked Comedy Central from my TV set and sent this article to all my friends. I'll bet you cowardly hypocrites wouldn't have the guts to show Muhammad in this situation.

Message: I find it not only blasphemous but extremely offensive that your Comedy Central Programming and Viacom allow Ms. Silverman the license to denigrate the beliefs of even marginally religious Christians and Jews. This is not humor—this is "hate speech" directed towards the Judeo-Christian community.

Message: I am absolutely disgusted by the lastest episode where it depicted Sarah having sex with a black "god". I can assure you I will no longer watch your network until you take such filth off the air. Not even South Park has gone this far before. It will be a sad day when Sarah stands before the Lord and has to account for what she has done.

Message: SO THIS NO TALENT JEW CAN MAKE FUN OF OR TRY TO EMBARRESS CHRISTIANS? AND SO IT GOES. I WANT HER TO BASH THE JEWISH RELIGION OR MUSLIM RELIGION. NO? WHY NOT? HOW MANY PRODUCERS DID SHE SLEEP WITH FOR THIS DUMBASS SHOW? OOPPSSS? HEY THE 1ST AMMENDMENT GOES BOTH WAYS . . . RIGHT NO TALENT SARAH?

Message: hi, that sarah silverman show is hilarious. it's amazing—the wonders of special effects nowadays. who would have thought you could take a monkey and make it act like it's humping a jew with words coming out of the monkey and everything. it looked so real. did she actually touch the monkey. did it bite her? she certainly is a brave woman. that monkey sure must have stunk. he looked stinky. what do you feed it? what an actress she is! bravo!!!

I'll take this opportunity to answer one of the most repeated questions: Why didn't I choose to depict Muhammad having sex? The answer is simple: I don't want to get blown up with explosives. I am afraid of angering Muslims, but not afraid of angering Jews and Christians, so I chose to depict the Judeo-Christian God instead. It seems extremely obvious to me, but so many people asked . . .

                    *   *   *

There's a strange coda to this story. For as much anger as the sex-with-God bit caused, there was an equal amount of praise. For people who loved the pilot, this part of the episode was their favorite. After the first season, so many fans would ask me, "Is God coming back??" The writers and I felt we owed it to the viewers, so we wrote an entire episode for HIM in season two. His buffoonery in this episode dwarfed that of his first appearance. He was desperate, needy, and clingy. He smoked weed, got paranoid and insecure, accidentally killed a man, pathetically covered it up, and took a completely cavalier attitude about it. He got sloppy drunk, made a fool of himself at my high school reunion, and tumbled down a cartoonishly long flight of stairs. I dumped him, after which he immediately begged to just sleep in my bed with me. Serious douche-chill-inducing stuff. And yet, we never heard a word about this episode—not a single letter. Maybe all those people who threatened to yank out their cable boxes after the pilot actually went through with it.

the SARAH SiLVERMAN PROGRAMME

Fax

To: J. SCHRAM   From: D. STERLING

Fax: _____   Pages: 3 TOTAL

Phone: _____   Date: _____

Re: _____   CC: _____

☐ Urgent   ☐ For Review   ☐ Please Comment   ☐ Please Reply   ☐ Please Recycle

● Comments:

PERSONAL &
CONFIDENTIAL

Sunset Gower Studios
1438 N. Gower Street , Box 30
Hollywood, CA 90028

The censors were nervous about a scene in which my character is asked for her driver's license and instead offers a shitty drawing of a penis. We had to clear the drawing with Standards before shooting. After receiving this fax, they asked us to lose the "demarcation of the head" and "shorten the pee hole." Note that our stationery at the time still reflected the show's original title, with the fancy French spelling of "Program."

June 13, 2006

FR: DAN STERLING
TO JESSICA SCHRAM

Dear Jessica

What do you think of this penis?

Best, DS

Mein Kampf, Part Five:
Writers' Guild Strike a Real Pain in the *Kampf*

I suspect that the show I turned in to Comedy Central is not quite the one they originally hoped for. My guess is that the show they really wanted was one in which I did stand-up and peppered it with a couple of sketches and songs, possibly all riffing on one overarching theme. That is pretty much what most of the network's other comedian-centered shows are like. It's a format that originally started with *The Man Show* and found wild success with Chappelle's show and *Mind of Mencia*. It's a show that's inexpensive and easy to produce in large quantities. Instead, I burdened them with a lavish show filled with union-wage workers, ensemble cast, stunts, special effects, visual effects, and animation.

Most network sitcoms churn out twenty-two or more episodes a year within a forty-week period, with almost no breaks. While the actors are downstairs shooting one week's episode, the writers are upstairs laboring frantically to get next week's script finished on time. Personally, I couldn't run my show like that and still maintain quality in writing or performance. I'm not saying it can't be done—it clearly can—I'm just saying *I* can't do it. For me it would be torture. Not "torture" like when the CIA extradites terror suspects to Yemen and the interrogators send 100,000 volts of electricity through their balls, but I'd be very grouchy.

The Sarah Silverman Program operates differently. We do the show one phase at a time. First we gather and write steadily—from 10:30 a.m. to 6:00 p.m., for three months. Together we pitch ideas for storylines, then figure out the detailed beats to each act (there are four acts per episode, divided by commercial breaks). Once an outline is completed, we usually assign the actual script to the writer who originally came up with the germ of the idea for the episode. Once written, Dan Sterling, Rob Schrab, and I will give notes. After the notes are addressed, Dan will do a final pass and make it perfect. Only once we've put a bow on all the scripts for the season do we begin shooting them.

I think our process has paid off. It's striking how often people visit us and remark on what a happy and fun place our set seems to be—and it is. My hope is that this happiness comes across to the viewer. Growing up, I loved seeing actors on screen who seemed to be enjoying their work in real life. Watching Dan Aykroyd and John Belushi on *Saturday Night Live*, I could feel their chemistry and delight in playing off each other. You could tell they were friends. It was the same thing with *The Carol Burnett Show*: My favorite part was when the cast members would crack each other up and knock the whole scene off the rails.

From the beginning, the network has expressed their frustrations with me about the production headaches and costs of my show, and I imagine that, by now, four years into it, there must be a secret little room at their corporate offices that contains nothing but a tile floor with a photo image of my face, and a urine drain right where my mouth is.

Because virtually everyone else who worked on the show was covered by a union except the writers, I asked for them to be unionized. They were talented and devoted, I couldn't do the show without them, and despite the increased production costs, they deserved the health care, pensions, and other basic protections that the guys who painted our sets enjoyed. Comedy Central stepped up, made a pact with the Writers' Guild, and began paying the writers union rates. Of course, just weeks after the writing staff unionized, the show was forced to shut down and join the devastating one-hundred-day writers' strike. Eep.

LEFT: *Writer "Tall Jon" Schroeder and me picketing during the writers' strike*
RIGHT: *Chris Romano atop Tall Jon with Dan Sterling crushed below*

The strike was brutal for Comedy Central, just as it was brutal for everyone else. The ones hurt the most from the strike were those who had nothing to gain from it—the people involved in every part of production, from wardrobe to lights to catering, were out of work with no hope of a silver lining.

Even after the strike ended, the tone throughout Hollywood had changed. Cost cutting was the order of the day, and few shows, even successful ones, were impervious to the new industry-wide paradigm. After our season finished airing, the network informed us that the only way the show could be renewed was if we cut the budget by 30 percent.

All of us—Rob Schrab, Dan Sterling, our other executive pro-

ducer, Heidi Herzon, and me—wanted to keep going with the series. In two seasons across the span of over two years, we had so far
produced only twenty-two episodes. We felt we were just beginning
to hit our stride creatively. So Rob, Dan, Heidi, and I agreed: We'd
find a way to deliver the show at nearly two-thirds the cost, assuming we could do it without turning it into a completely insulting
piece of shit.

*Writer Jon Schroeder and head writer Dan Sterling. Tall Jon lost a bet
with* Jimmy Kimmel Live *head writer Gary Greenberg over when the
strike would end and happily wore this carefully chosen outfit for the day.
We were all excited to be back at work.*

For six weeks, we crunched numbers and explored endless scenarios. We begged the unions to give us a break on wage hikes, but they wouldn't budge. Comedy Central suggested we produce the show more like broadcast networks do it—write and shoot the show *simultaneously* as opposed to *successively*—because that would make it faster and therefore cheaper. But it also would have made it impossible for me to be in the writers' room. Look, I know the show is retarded, but much of that retardedness comes from my retarded head. Not to brag.

The network's most repeated demand was that we shoot more weeks in a row with fewer hiatuses. It's not a crazy demand—it's how most shows are done and it would have saved tons of money—*faster is cheaper*. But seriously, I would have fucking died. I was born with many advantages in life, but boundless energy and an ironclad immune system were not among them. Had we compressed the shooting schedule, I would have gotten sick, my performance in every capacity would have suffered greatly, and worst of all, I'd have become a gigantic cunt. I didn't want to disappoint my partners in crime, but I had no choice. I had to hold fast to the principles Garry Shandling had instilled in me years before: understanding my limits, and taking on only as much as I could without compromising quality of work or life.

After six weeks, we still couldn't make the budget. The network somehow managed to scrape up a little more money, but we were warned that this was the absolute end of the road.

Rob, Dan, Heidi, and I were all so stressed and exhausted from weeks of banging our heads against the wall—none of us could figure out how to do the show within the given budget. We agreed that there would be better things down the road for all of us, and that the universe was sending us a message: It was time for the show to end. I drafted an e-mail to Comedy Central and ran it by the others. They told me to send it:

From: Sarah Silverman

Date: February 26, 2009 4:59:39 PM PST
Subject: FROM SARAH, DAN, ROB AND HEIDI.

Lauren Doug and Gary,
We are going around and around, fighting over cuts, and it's awful. We love this show too much to do it this way. We'd rather end it now having done 22 perfect shows we are so proud of than grind out shows we don't believe in only to be hidden with no promotion 14 months after we last aired. We have to like ourselves enough to believe we will work again, and this isn't what we have to settle for. It's not about the money, if it was we would have never been here. It's the quality. Thank you so much for all your effort. I know you guys did all you could to get us what you did. We just can't make it work. We can't make a boot out of a sandal.

So sadly, Sarah, Dan, Rob and Heidi

It was over.

The next day, Comedy Central asked us if we could do the show if they added a little more to the budget, but we still didn't think it was enough to do it without significantly compromising quality. We could have made *a* television show with the money they were offering, but it wouldn't look anything like the one we had been making. We sent another e-mail:

From: Sarah Silverman

Sent: Sat, 28 Feb 2009 4:39 pm
Subject: FROM US AGAIN . . .

Lauren, Doug and Gary,
There's no need to repeat what was said in our last e-mail, but it all still
stands. We know you are strapped. But if you really want to know what it
would take for us to have any desire to come back, it would be if we had the
same budget as last year. No more, just the same. We are assuming this
will be a no go, and we're prepared for that, but that's what it would take
to make it worth it. After seven months of waiting to be picked up and then
the evisceration of our budget, we have totally lost our boners for doing
this show and are more excited about the thought of what could be next
for us. It's just not enticing to change the show from this wonderful thing
to a sketchy looking stage show. Television series that completely retool
midstream never, ever work, unless they bring in Ted McGinley, which was
the next inevitable step for us.
Assuming we are moving on, we will do so with all the great memories and
pride of having done an amazing show.
Thank you so much for everything.

Love, Sarah Rob Dan and Heidi

The next day we were informed that Lauren Corrao (the West
Coast president of the network at that time) had supposedly come
up with a plan to save the show. She had worked out a deal with
LOGO, the gay-oriented network within the MTV Networks
group of cable channels, to subsidize the rest of the money needed
for our production costs in exchange for the right to broadcast our
first reruns. That meant we were pretty much looking at the budget
we'd had for the previous season. It was still a net reduction with
the various expense increases, but it was manageable.

Within a few weeks we were back in the writers' room, laughing our heads off, more excited than ever about the show. The gays had saved us.

I Literally Work with a Bunch of Dicks. By That, I Mean That There Are Actual Penises Everywhere I Look. Seriously.

Kevin Nealon once spent an hour hanging out in the *TSSP* writers' room. As he was leaving, he turned to me.

"This group reminds me of a real Harvard crew," referring to the *Harvard Lampoon*–bred writers that populate *SNL* and *30 Rock* and *Frasier* and such. I was so proud.

"Really??"

He looked at me as if I was completely insane. "No."

All of the foregoing drama about the show's near demise might have suggested that what we were fighting to save was a precious, delicate cultural treasure, crafted by some historic gathering of extraordinary wits and talents, not seen since the Algonquin Round Table. But as Kevin will tell you, that is not the case. The *TSSP* writers are sick, depraved fucks, and I don't say that with bravado. I don't think being a sick, depraved fuck is necessarily the path to comedy immortality. I just happen to love these particular sick fucks, and I love the fact that our cramped little writers' room is a sanctuary, a place where you are not only safe, but encouraged, to completely indulge your primal instincts. In that way, it's like the opposite of most jobs.

This unprofessional behavior was established on day one when writer (and recurring cast member) Chris Romano's penis made its first appearance. Chris is a small, sweet, lean, frenetic, baby-faced monkey of a man. He has no social filter, no sense of physical, medical, or economic danger, and a thick New Hampshire accent. (Shockingly, he's from Nashua, the next town over from where I grew up, though we didn't meet until Rob and Dan Harmon brought him and his writing partner, Eric Falconer, onto the show.) Chris rubs his crotch on everything, animate and inanimate, his bosses included, regardless of whether they're in the mood for it. He is the funniest person I have ever met in my entire life, and it just so happens that one of the main ways he expresses himself is by taking his penis out of his pants. For Chris, it's an especially bold move, because his penis, to put it delicately, does not have an imposing presence; it's really more the *promise* of a penis. I don't claim that this habit of his is witty or original, but every time he pulls out his cock, it strikes me as hilarious. If for no other reason than that *he* seems to get so much pleasure from it. And to be fair, Chris does it as cleverly as anyone possibly could. For example, he'll walk into the room with his penis poking through a hole in the center of a paper napkin, and gleefully declare in his New Hampshire brogue, "My dick just ate lob-stah."

The fact that I laugh at this kind of thing has consequences, of course. It explicitly encourages such behavior, signaling not just that it's acceptable, but actually *preferable*. Because the truth about all this phallic mischief is that it slows down the writing process. In fact, slowing down the writing process is the whole point. Figuring out how to structure a satisfying story is a gigantic headache, and often not much fun. The gratification only comes many months later when the episodes finally air, whereas pulling down your pants is immediately rewarding.

One thing about writers: We tend to be lazy as shit, but become very motivated in pursuit of a joke. Case in point, the morning we were to move into our new offices, Chris Romano and his writing partner, Eric Falconer, woke up extra early. They broke into Rob's sparkling new office, and with the teamwork that made them such stars in our writers' room, Falconer took a gigantic shit in Rob's toilet. I don't know what he did with the toilet paper, because there was none present in the bowl. This is called "love of your craft." Needless to say, the bowel movement was not flushed. Instead, Romano placed on it a hand-made flag made from toothpick and napkin, on which was written, simply, "I know what you did last summer."

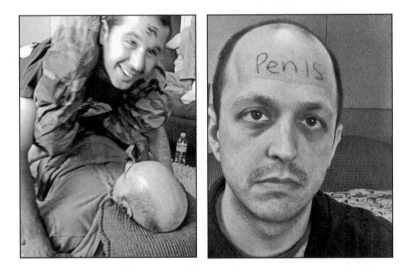

LEFT: *Romano let me draw a swastika on his forehead, and I let him rape executive producer-writer-creator-director Rob Schrab.*
RIGHT: *I asked Dan if he wanted to join the "Pen 15" club. He did.*

*Every season we end up spending the first two or three weeks
of writing in my apartment before we can find office space.*

The costs of doing business this way go beyond mere distraction. One of them, especially over a period of years, is a complete loss of perspective. Example: At the end of the writing phase for season three, Harris Wittels took a job writing for NBC's *Parks and Recreation*. It was an enormous step up in income, and a chance to work for a major network, and with the amazing and adorable Amy Poehler. We were all so excited for him. To mark his first day of work, we ordered a huge bouquet of corny balloons and made a gigantic collage of all the photos we had of him with his penis out, and had the whole thing delivered to his new studio offices. It was our way of saying *We're rooting for you, pal*—and to let his new colleagues know a little bit about their newly hired collaborator. Harris, however, intercepted the collage and stashed it in his office before anyone could see it.

A few weeks later, I called Harris to see how it was going. Afterward, I joined Rob Schrab and Dan Sterling in a meeting and gave them the scandalous report:

"Harris says he's having a great time at *Parks and Rec*, but he said he feels like if he farted or took out his penis he'd be fired."

Dan looked at me and asked me to really think about what I just said. "Is there any job, other than this one, in which that would *not* be the case?"

He was right, of course. I had totally forgotten that we all turned into fucking animals in that room.

LEFT: *On a conference call with the network, I started scratching Dan's head, which puts him in a semitrance. I was able to write this, take a picture of it with my phone, and e-mail it to him without his noticing. Watching him open this e-mail was one of my prouder moments.*

RIGHT: *Dan is smart and uses big words like "balaclava" and "buttressed," and he is tortured by us for it, as illustrated by this new cereal created by Rob Schrab.*

Writer Chelsea Peretti left her hair clip in the writers' room. We took this picture and e-mailed it to her (down the hall in her office) with the subject heading, "Did you leave this in the writers' room?" Note: This is writer Harris Wittels's penis. I wouldn't want him to go uncredited here. (His parents are so proud right now!!)

There might have been a microscopic trace of resentment in Dan's query. He's the one who suffers most from the relentless childishness and perversion. As head writer, it's his job to keep the discussion in the room going, and to deliver outlines and scripts on schedule. The joy on my face when the writers pull down their pants or faux-rape each other is matched in intensity by the heartbreak on Dan's. It's hard to be the killjoy, the guy whose job it is to stop the laughter, and nowhere is this truer than in a room full of comedy writers.

I should mention that among this handful of writers there were two women, equally as nuts. There was Chelsea Peretti, who took a pregnancy test on her first day of work and shared the pee-drenched result with us as it materialized. And, of course, there was I, who remained at all times a perfect lady, with the possible exception of once peeing (just a tiny bit) on the rug in Dan's office, and one time exposing just the very tippy-top of my pubes.

Dan has a nearly permanent look of agony on his face, relies heavily on sleeping pills, and, in the four years we've worked together, has lost almost all of his hair. The fact that he's the "mature" one, cast as the bad cop on the staff, is especially ironic because he is arguably the most disturbed one among us. Dan reads the *New York Times* and effortlessly spouts words like "perspicacious," but when it comes to putting farts and doody into the scripts, he has less restraint, less reverence for "Make It a Treat," than anyone on the staff. As much as he's the one who has to keep us on track and maintain our focus, my favorite part of Dan is that he is by far the hardest laugher of all of us. There is no better way to nurture comedy than watching tears of laughter run down your boss's face, and he offers that in abundance.

After the first season of *TSSP*, it wasn't clear when or if we'd be picked up for another season. So when Dan was offered a job running *The Daily Show with Jon Stewart*, he took it. A couple of months later, I called him in New York and asked how it was going. The job was very exciting, he said, but I heard something wistful in his voice. In what seemed to be a lament, he added, "No one farts here." But pretty soon, *TSSP* did get renewed for a second season. Dan moved back to L.A. and got a face full of what he'd been missing.

*   *   *

After fifteen years of making my living in stand-up, *The Sarah Silverman Program* has been a lesson in collaboration. Rob, Dan, and I live by the mantra "Whoever is most passionate." If I was mentoring someone, that's the Shandling-esque advice I would proffer: Find people you really respect and trust, and then at each decision, heed the most passionate voice. I love that because it eliminates nearly all struggle. And when you're doing a show that's mostly about farts, penises, and vaginas, there should be as little struggle as possible.

THE SECOND-MOST-IMPORTANT THING IN LIFE: LOVE

At the time that this book is being written, I am single. If you've ever heard that song by Beyoncé, "Single Ladies," I am one of the people she's singing about. I have to be, because she sings, "*All the single ladies.*" If she didn't mean to include me in that, then she really needs to choose her words more carefully.

I was recently dating a man, but it's over. His name was Ronald, and he seemed like a serious candidate, but he said that he couldn't get past his allergy to my cat. I insisted that I didn't have a cat, but he refused to believe me. He held that the cat's name was Dorothy, and that it was a French Short-Whiskered Nectarine Hunter. This infuriated me. I would never name my cat Dorothy, nor would I name it anything else, unless it actually existed, which it doesn't. Also, I looked at the Cat Fanciers' Association official registry of pedigreed cats, and there's no such thing as a French Short-Whiskered Nectarine Hunter.

Still, I felt that Ronald and I had something special, something worth fighting for. I went to see him and explained that I'd taken Dorothy to an animal shelter, and that they had immediately euthanized her. I added that they took serious sadistic pleasure in it, and that the process of her execution was long enough and painful enough that Dorothy was no doubt forced to reflect on the anguish she'd caused in her life. I told Ronald that I watched the cremation of Dorothy's corpse until the final bits of her bone turned to ash, just to make sure there was no chance of my man ever being sickened by that animal again.

And while none of that was true, I did take steps in real life to make sure Ronald felt attended to in the relationship, allergy-wise. I had actually taken a new apartment, burned all of my clothes and bought all new ones, and traded in my old mattress for one of those spaceship-y foam ones. He was impressed with my efforts, but he still hesitated. He said that he suddenly realized it wasn't his cat allergy that bothered him about me. I asked if he was sure. He said he was, and he pointed to an enormous, morbidly obese Himalayan that lounged on his couch. It was so coated in dander flakes that it reminded me of the sugar-dusted fruit tarts at the café near the apartment I had lived in until 10:00 a.m. I was angry and hungry. All this time, he had a cat! I was also fairly sexed-up, and this fact just made me angrier. Here I was with this very immediate bodily need, and our relationship was in such a state that it would take us forever to ramp up into sex. All the fighting and crying and negotiating and manipulating that we'd have to go through before we could make an organic segue to intercourse—it could have taken hours.

I was beginning to suspect he wasn't being honest with me about his reasons for wanting to end our relationship. Can you imagine a guy actually behaving like this? I did not get into the romance business to have some guy avoid saying hurtful things to me. I'm sorry to sound cruel, but his behavior was exactly like Adolf Hitler's. I left Ronald's apartment, went home, and simultaneously dined, cried, and masturbated. In the midst of doing that, I also laughed. And then I thought, *What the hell do I need a man for anyway?* Everything that I enjoy, I seem to be able to do with two hands, a fork, and an iPhone.*

But that kind of thinking is hackneyed and glib. And there is one thing that I really, really like to have company for. Watching TV. I'm not particularly needy in relationships, I actually demand a fair amount of space. But I really like to be in bed with another human being and watch TV. That's as intimate and reassuring and tender as it gets for me. I find dating exhausting and uninteresting, and I really would like to skip over the hours of conversation that you need just to get up to speed on each other's lives, and the stories I've told a million times. I just want to get to the watching TV in bed. If you're on a date with me, you can be certain that this is what I'm evaluating you for—how good is it going to be, cuddling with you in bed and watching *Damages*? I'm also looking to see if you have clean teeth. For me, anything less than very clean teeth is fucking disgusting.

Here's what I would like to do: I would like to get into bed with a DVD of *Damages* and have a line of men cue up at my door. I would station a dental hygienist at the front of the line who would examine the men's teeth. Upon passing inspection, she (I've never met a male hygienist, and neither have you) would send them back to my bedroom, one at time, in intervals of ten minutes, during which I would cuddle with them and watch *Damages*. Leaving nothing to chance, using some sort of medical telemetry, I would have a clinician take basic readings of my heart rate and brain waves, and create a comparison chart to illustrate which candidate was the

---

* *I may or may not have made up this story.*

most soothing presence for me. After reviewing all the data from what will now be known in diagnostic manuals throughout the world as the Silverman-*Damages*-Nuzzle-Test, I will make my selection. And, of course, soon thereafter, we will make love in a similar fashion to mentally diseased animals on a meth binge.

JEW

I don't remember if I mentioned this to you before, but I am Jewish. If my publisher had a sense of decency, they would have printed that disclaimer prominently on the book cover. Otherwise, how would you necessarily know? I mean I can't think of anything about me that really says "Jew!!" I even once spent a few weeks in Fjarðabyggð, Iceland, and blended in with the Nordic Gentile population seamlessly—although there *was* an incident in which an intoxicated Icelandic shepherd mistook my thick black hair for a scouring pad and tried to use it to scrub off the fermented shark meat he had earlier vomited onto the antlers of his reindeer. But you know how Icelandic shepherds can be—they're big-picture guys. They can't make much sense of what's right in front of their faces.

So I'm sorry if you're just putting it together now—that I am Jewish. It's just not fun to be reading and thoroughly enjoying a book and then you get close to the end and discover that the thing was written by a member of an ethnicity that disgusts you. I write this chapter somewhat begrudgingly. To be honest, I would like to go about my life exploiting the subject of Jewishness for comedy, and not be saddled with the responsibility to actually represent, defend, or advance the cause of the Jewish people. Nevertheless, my Jew editor convinced me to write a chapter on Jewiness by using one of our culture's greatest tools of persuasion: relentless nagging.

As religions go, I do think Judaism is one of the better ones. Jews don't ring my doorbell and shove pamphlets in my face. They aren't pushy. Let me clarify: Jews aren't pushy about their *religion*. That is what Jews are not pushy about. Their religion.

Another nice thing about the Jews is that their rabbis don't make a habit of sexually violating their youngest and most vulnerable congregants. Of course, there are obvious reasons for this. For one thing, Jewish clergy are allowed to fuck and masturbate and marry. The first two of these activities work amazingly well for relieving sexual tension. (See "Sarah Silverman's Secret Tips for Relieving Sexual Tension.") Oh, also, Jewish clergy are allowed to have vaginas. As a general rule for any large organization, if you're looking to reduce the rape-iness of it, try hiring more women. But most importantly, at least in the Orthodox world, Jewish children—and all members of the clan—are not exactly asking for it, clothing-wise. Orthodox Jewish men in my neighborhood wear large black hats with round brims, or if they don't have one of those on their heads, they wear what I can only describe as "furry tires"—white stockings that go all the way up their calves, and black culottes-type things that balloon from the end of their white stockings up to their waists, where they are often met by a stringy beard which one can only pray does not contain remnants of creamed herring. The women generally sport shawls or scarves around their heads, with long, black dresses dropping shapelessly to their ankles. I wouldn't even hump the thigh of someone in this kind of getup. Also, I live in Southern California. It's a *desert* and they're all covered literally from head to toe in black. There's not a lot in modern Muslim orthodoxy that I'm a fan of, but at least they know how to dress for their local climate.

So where is this coming from historically or scripturally? I don't recall Jesus, King of the Jews, wearing a furry hat and white stockings. He looked very climate-appropriate in his cotton tunic and sandals, just a Hacky Sack away from modern Cali garb. But he did die in unspeakable agony with nails in his hands as blood slowly trickled out of his body. It's hard to have it all, I guess.

Jews also don't seem to believe in Hell. That's a nifty feature for a faith. I mean, if there were a store where you could literally shop for a religion, and on the shelf you saw two basic choices: one in which, if you have an orgasm caused by anyone other than your opposite-sex spouse, you will spend eternity having to use fire as toilet paper; and another that allows you any kind of orgasm you want, with the only possible downside being the additional effort you might have to make on laundry day—you're going with option two. Of course, some people need Hell. If you're the type of guy who sees a hooker in an alleyway and instinctively thinks, *Hey, now there's something I could rape and kill without any consequences*, then the concept of Hell might really keep you out of trouble.

New Hampshire:
Where Cows Are Well Done, and Jews Are Rare

I have no religion. I grew up in a non-observant household, in what I would guess to be the least Jewish of the contiguous forty-eight states. You might argue for something like Texas or Oklahoma, but both states have deserts and dry weather, and Texas has several major metropolitan centers—serious Jew bait. Arkansas, Tennessee, and Kentucky are pretty damned un-Semitic, but New Hampshire has arctic weather, and both bears and moose, and if you know anything about Jews, you know they're not comfortable with large game.

Growing up, the only way I really sensed I was a Jew was by dint of the fact that everyone around me was *not*. My dark features and name both scream "Jew" like an air-raid siren. Most people in New Hampshire have names like Lisa Bedard (pronounced *Beh-daahhd*) or Cheryl Dubois (*Doo-boyz*). I was the only one with hairy arms and "gorilla legs." In third grade, Matt Italia threw pennies and nickels at my feet as I stepped onto the bus. (That wasn't as bad as it sounds. I ended up going out with Matt Italia. Plus, I made 52 cents!) But I don't think Matt or the other kids were expressing hate. I think they were just trying to wrap their heads around the differences between people. Matt didn't hate me when he threw change at my feet any more than he loved me when we were boyfriend and girlfriend.

Recently Miley Cyrus got herself in trouble when a photograph was taken of her making "Chinese eyes," right next to one of her Asian friends (see photograph opposite). I have trouble believing that hate of the Asian people is what inspired her to do that. I think it was just young kids making levity of their differences. I'd go almost so far as to say that it was perfectly healthy. If there had not been an Asian kid in that picture, the "Chinese eyes" gesture would have seemed random and uncalled for. Also, in more practical terms, it's just so easy to tug slightly at the corners of your eyes. With black friends it's much more of a logistical challenge. You'd have to find some shoe polish or a giant sausage, and what teenage girl with two simultaneous show business careers has that kind of time? Miley was a girl with no options.

Seriously, Though, New Hampshire Was Not Especially Jewish

Until I moved to New York City after high school, the only Jews I really knew were related to me. After Saturday-night sleepovers I'd go to church on Sundays with my Christian friends and their families far more than I ever went to temple. But both places of worship seemed to be these bizarre forums where authority figures told fucked-up ghost stories between spurts of loving encouragement.

In case I haven't yet sufficiently illustrated for you just how un-Jewish New Hampshire was, let me put it this way: The only day care my mother could find for me was at a convent.

When I was seven years old, my parents did what was fashion-able and got divorced. In addition to creating me, it's something they did for which I'm eternally grateful. Their divorce should be a model for us all; they both remarried happily, and all four spouses became good friends. I am entirely serious when I tell you that my stepmother, Janice, sends my father to my mother's house bimonthly to get his toenails clipped. (My father is apparently unable to do such tasks himself, and Janice is entirely grossed out by the idea.)

This is not to say that the divorce wasn't disruptive at the out-set. My sisters moved in with my dad, and my mom went back to college—two scenarios that now strike me as perfectly acceptable templates for ABC sitcoms.

1980: Mom graduates college and I get a new hat.

From the end of the schoolday until my mother finished her classes in early evening, I was cared for at a local convent. Though "cared for" might be a slight misnomer. I've had some wonderful experiences with nuns in my life, but these weren't among them.

At naptime, we were instructed to lie down on floor mats, and expected to fall asleep immediately. Anyone caught with eyes open or, God forbid, talking, got smacked. Actually smacked. So I lay on my mat, eyes clenched shut, terrified that they would sense I was still awake. Trying to get kids to sleep by scaring the shit out of them seems so obviously paradoxical in hindsight. Still, I'm sympathetic to the nuns' violent impulses. I mean, if I'd given up sex to devote myself to a man who I had to just *trust* loved me, despite never being physically around to prove it, I'd probably be smacking little children too.

Every day the nuns would take us on a nature walk during which they would distribute peanut-butter-and-jelly sandwiches cut in four squares. They demanded that we eat every crumb or else—the "or else" being, you guessed it, violence. I reiterate that this constant threat of brutality was a new cultural experience. Up to then, in my Jewy home, I'd only been exposed to passive aggression, or the threat of being viewed as a disappointment, max.

But my prolonged state of anxiety caused my tiny mind to play dark tricks on me. You know how your brain will fuck with you? Like when you are masturbating and it goes and throws an image of your mom or dad or nana into the mix? It was like I had this bully living in my mind that scared the shit out of me. It's like when you're walking and you tell yourself, "If I don't clear that crack in the pavement by the time this car passes me, I'll die." That same bully convinced me that the jelly in each square of PB&J the nuns gave me was, without a doubt, their period blood. I would take little bites and gag violently as I chewed and swallowed, only slightly more afraid of getting hit than of ingesting the sisters' monthly menses.

Lest you think I share this story as some sort of broad attack on the Catholic Church, I'll inform you that I spent the better part of six years sharing a bed with a God-fearing Roman Catholic. Though that last sentence does come off a little *some-of-my-best-friends-are-black*-ish, now that I'm rereading it.

Unlike Jesus Christ, I Am Embraced, Rather Than Murdered, by Jews, for Flapping My Yapper

Despite Donald and Beth Ann Silverman's relative indifference to their ancestral faith, Jewishness would become, in one way or another, a large theme for their children. My sister Susie not only became a rabbi, she married a man named Yosef Abramowitz, making her name Susan Silverman Abramowitz. When I was on *SNL*, I did a bit about this for "Weekend Update," in which I suggested that my sister and her husband just rename themselves "The Jews." Then they wrote a book called *Jewish Family and Life: Traditions, Holidays and Values for Today's Parents and Children*. At this point you might ask—maybe more rhetorically than out of genuine curiosity— How much more Jewish can a person get? Well, my answer to you, madam or sir, would be: Quite a bit more. Because Susie and her husband moved to Israel. To live on a kibbutz. Take that, secular New England upbringing!

Susie pursued her religion doggedly, but in my case, the faith has sort of pursued me. At the very least we met in the middle and developed a mutually beneficial relationship. I have been deemed "good for the Jews" and from that there seems to be no going back; the Jews have spoken. I could do anything now and I'd still be considered good for them. I could, for example, accept Jesus as my lord and savior. I could deny the Holocaust. I mean, when you think about it, the proof isn't exactly overwhelming—what, a couple trendy arm tattoos and some survivor testimonials filmed by Steven Spielberg? Um, Steven Spielberg? The guy who made *E.T.*?

I believe the reasons I'm beloved by Jews are twofold. First, I'm known for making graphic jokes about sex and scatological matters. Jews, by and large, are comfortable with sexuality—they are just as encouraging of recreational sex as they are of sex for procreation (though maybe a little more so of the latter, since that's how grandchildren are made). Also, many Jews cannot be stopped from discussing what goes on in their GI tracts—the GI tract of a Jew over age twenty-three is true melodrama reminiscent of the Old Testament: sudden mass exodus, long arduous journeys, floods, futility, agony, questioning God's wisdom, and lactose intolerance. So the things I talk about are not blasphemy to Jewish people.

Secondly, I became somewhat of a public figure—a visibly Jewish one. I look Jewish, I have a hard time containing my opinions, and I find it very difficult to get through the day without getting a stain of some kind on my shirt. Also, my last name combines a precious metal with the word "man." Jews love any Jewish public figure. "You know that serial killer, Son of Sam? Jewish!" When the Clinton-Lewinsky scandal broke, I wasn't happy that our president had an affair, but I was kind of tickled to bits that it was with this sassy, chubby Jewess. Even expressions of outright anti-Semitism can be good for the Jews. Bless Mel Gibson for his drunken rant about Jews this and Jews that; here was something you could point to as evidence that Jew-hating isn't just some abstract concept in the ether. It exists here and now, even right out in the open. Besides, in America, where Jews represent only 2.2 percent of the population, I guess any press is good press.

I talk about being Jewish in my act more than I'm really entitled to, considering that I'm an agnostic at best who has no background of participation in Jewish traditions other than nausea. I've, in fact, been making Jew jokes from an early age, and like most of the jokes I made as a kid, this was largely a defense mechanism. The smart fat kid will be the first to make a fat joke as protection from whatever insults the other kids might hurl at him, and, as a smart Jew, I did likewise. Joking about my differentness seemed to put the people around me at ease. Even though I actually knew almost nothing about being a Jew other than that I *was* one.

Nag-ative Campaigning

Besides warning the reader that this author is a Jew, the other thing that should have been printed on the cover of this book is that I, Sarah Silverman, saved the world. And it was with relatively little effort. I pretty much just sat on my couch and took care of the matter while a PA ran to pick up my lunch. I hope that doesn't sound cocky.

In the event you don't know what I'm talking about, let me explain: I gave you President Barack Obama. You're welcome. I don't know if his presidency will actually save the world, but at least now when you travel internationally and people ask, you can say, "I'm from the United States," while looking straight into their eyes instead of at the laces of your Pumas. And to be totally honest, it was a joint effort between George W. Bush and me. I'm not sure our country would have made the leap to elect a black president if we hadn't had two terms of a mentally handicapable white one.

I fell in love with Obama during the 2008 campaign. Actually, I started falling for him four years earlier, just after the 2004 election when I saw him on *Letterman*. Dave asked Obama where he thought Kerry went wrong, and he laughed, replying, "Oh I don't know. Maybe windsurfing wasn't the most accessible publicity sport? Maybe he could have played a little softball instead?"

I wanted to contribute to the campaign effort but didn't see an effective way to do it. I figured anyone who cared what I thought would most likely be planning to vote for Obama anyway.

But in September of 2008, I got a call from Mik Moore and Ari Wallach, a couple of activists who had formed an organization called JewsVote. They explained that the most reliable voting bloc in the electoral jackpot of Florida is elderly Jews. They're not the demographic majority, but they all vote. This gives them power way out of proportion to their numbers. And the elderly Jews of Florida, the guys said, were *not* planning to vote for Barack Hussein Obama, the disconcertingly young black man with the oddly, Muslim-ish background and murky level of commitment to Israel. BUT virtually all of their grandchildren *were* planning to vote for him.

So Mik and Ari hatched an idea for a campaign called "The Great Schlep." It was brilliant—optimistic and delightfully manipulative. Its core aim was to exploit the outsized fondness Jewish elders have for their grandchildren, and harness that power to win Florida for Obama. The Great Schlep would urge the grandchildren of Jewish geezers to get down to Florida, dispel their grandparents' misguided fears of the black man with the funny name, and convince them to vote for him.

Like everyone else working in the Obama movement, Mik and Ari saw digital media as a critical tool. And they thought of me after seeing the success of a video I made for my then-boyfriend, Jimmy Kimmel, called *I'm Fucking Matt Damon*. (Thank you, thank you so much. No, please, sit.) I loved the notion that I could help by encouraging the generation who was already planning to vote for Obama to persuade their elders to do the same. But I warned Mik and Ari that, as excited as I was to do it, they needed to lower their expectations. I reminded them that the enormous popularity of *Fucking Matt Damon* could be attributed mostly to (a) huge movie star Matt Damon, and (b) *fucking*. Neither of which had much to do with me. Also, that video really had no message or social purpose, nor did it have any great effect other than to make people honk their horns at me and yell, "Hey, are you still fucking Matt Damon?"

I wasn't sure that making a video for the Great Schlep's Web site would really be all that effective, but at least it was something I knew how to do. They gave me no restrictions, just factual bullet points to include, like the name of the Web site and how to get involved. Beyond that I could do whatever I wanted. So I enlisted Dan Sterling, head writer and EP on *TSSP*, and we banged out a script. Wayne McClammy (amazing director of *I'm Fucking Matt Damon*, as well as many episodes of *The Sarah Silverman Program*) came aboard to collaborate and direct.

There was one other stipulation made by Mik and Ari: At some point in the video, I had to direct viewers to the Web site JewsVote .com. I felt this was unwise and told them so. If they wanted this video to go "viral," as I assumed they did, the very name "JewsVote" threatened to shrink the playing field by associating itself with an organization that implied only Jews would be welcome there. Of course, the campaign *was*, on one level, a call specifically to Jews, but at its heart it was a call to everyone. I was not comfortable promoting something so exclusionary in its language.

With just enough money to cover costs, we shot *The Great Schlep* video in my apartment, in the space of one morning with a nearly all-volunteer crew. The video largely consisted of me sitting on my couch talking to the camera. Appearances by Alex Desert and Dorothy Guise, and Wayne's visual style gave the piece vibrancy.

Fancypants journalistic institutions like the *New York Times* speculated that *The Great Schlep* might have been a decisive factor in Obama's Florida victory. I find that hard to believe, though I have to admit that sometimes I cite said fancypants articles when I am trying to get laid and it's looking iffy. Thanks for the orgasms, Frank Rich! (KIDDING—guys aren't impressed with good press, though combine that with some sweet big naturals and you got something. Fine—not *big*, per se, but I'd confidently say I at least have naturals you wouldn't sneeze at.)

Regardless of what I actually accomplished for the Obama campaign, I can tell you that I did *plenty* for my relationship with the Jews. And it's not because my message in the video was pro-Jew. It wasn't. It was a scold to the Jews whose ignorance and irrational fears made them blind to the potential of the man behind the funny name. But still they ate it up because what they saw was a visibly Jewish, somewhat familiar woman saying words like "Schlep" and "Jew" and "grandparent" in a loving manner. To say that I now can do no wrong in their eyes would not quite be an understatement, but I would say it's at least exactly accurate.

The Vatican Is Great. For Me to Poop On.

Well, it's nice to have a home with the Jews. No matter how disgustingly I behave in public, no matter what I say for or against the religion, they seem to accept me.

I have not been as reliably successful with Gentiles.

In the summer of '09, I was struck with an idea for a new video. I called it *Sell the Vatican, Feed the World*. It was so simple, and to me so unarguable. I wasn't speaking as a Jew, but as a person with eyes and ears. To me, the Vatican is an incomprehensibly extravagant and flamboyant headquarters for an institution that purports to promote humility and commitment to the needy. It's an actual city, teeming with hundreds of millions of dollars of treasure. I imagined what a huge and heartening change it would make if the Catholic Church cashed all that out and fed the whole world with it. If they actually did that, *I'd* probably join the church.

I knew *Sell the Vatican, Feed the World* wasn't gonna be for everyone, but what surprised me was how many critics viewed the piece specifically as a message from a *Jew*. Here's a sampling of the negative e-mail and good old-fashioned Jew-hatin' that the video elicited:

This jew should have burnt in an oven.

not sure if i should laugh my ass off or tell the jew whore to burn in hell . . .

fuck you you stupid, jewish, unfunny dumb cunt. take ur anti-american comments and shove them up ur nasty twat.

she is a jew and she is talking about selling the vatican??? why dont we ask your ppl to pay money since they are rich ms BIG SCREEN TV . . . instead of buying a tv maybe you should have a nose job.

you JEW has no right to speak about the vatican and the pope, speak about your own fucking religious institutes Pinocchio. And for the record, even though she is obviously (in my opinion) a formerly molested child (hence the fucked up views of the world), now that she is over 30, and hot, I wouldnt mind throwin 'it in her.

dear sarah silverman, please go kill yourself. you're ugly to look at and your jokes are not funny. You try a little too hard and its just not working. just go kill yourself please. quit wasting our oxygen!

This is why i fucking hate jews. They demand things that belong to
someone else to be sold and use it for the greater good and take all the
credit for it. Fuck, Hitler had the right idea.

Bill Donahue, president of the Catholic League, issued a statement:

*Silverman's filthy diatribe would never be allowed if the chosen target were
the Chief Rabbi of Jerusalem and the state of Israel.*

That might have been a keen point if I hadn't just done my previous video, *The Great Schlep*, which *was* directed at Jews, and where in
it I literally tell them to *"get off [their] fat Jewish asses."*

And so I have finally come to understand that whatever I say, I
should at least consider that some will view it through the filter of
my Jewishness. That said, I'm really fine with the above hate mail,
and there is a strong likelihood that, somewhere down the road, I
will remark again on the papacy and the Vatican. It's an enormous
target, both physically and intellectually, and I don't like to work
too hard.

A Nose by Any Other Name

Winona Ryder was born Winona Horowitz but she changed it.
What a classic sneaky Jew move.

I have a Jewy last name and I would never think to change it, but I
totally get Winona's choice. With a name like "Horowitz," you're no
longer an actress, you're a *Jewish* actress. Just like I'm "Jewish comedian
Sarah Silverman." For an actor, any modifier like that immediately

creates limitations. Think of what the word "character" does when placed before "actor." It denies that actor access to nearly all leading roles. You never hear "White actress Reese Witherspoon . . ." Eh. That's probably an old observation but it's true. I have comic friends who are gay. Some remain in the closet, and I don't blame them. It's not just out of fear of prejudice—it's fear of the gay community taking ownership of them. Suddenly, they are a gay comic, saddled with the responsibility to represent.

I have polled various show-businessy friends about Winona Ryder. I ask, "If Winona Ryder was Winona Horowitz, would she have been the star of *Edward Scissorhands* and *Age of Innocence* and all those elegant ingénue roles?" They all said no. All of them. I didn't expect that. I thought I was going into the discussion as the cynical one. *Jesus.*

"Silverman," I say quite subjectively, is less ethnic and more graceful than "Horowitz." There is the added advantage that Silverman alliterates with "Sarah" and therefore sounds more catchy. Maybe for that reason alone, I never felt the temptation to rename myself. It's hard for me to imagine that Jon Stewart would wield the same power if he had kept Liebowitz. Under his anglicized nom de show business, he talks almost nonstop about his Jewishness, but still, I think it would be different if he was doing so as Jon Liebowitz.

Whether I like it or not, I am, at least from the world's point of view, Jewish. And yes, I admit I draw on my Jewishness when comedically advantageous, though nothing I have ever done, or plan to do, will be about advancing any kind of Jewish agenda. But as it turns out, I cannot have it both ways. Because I have accepted being identified as Jewish, I'll also have to accept the responsibilities, limitations, and consequences. If I ever want to get away from that, it'll be an uphill battle that will require, among other things, a larynx transplant and some major hair removal.

AFTERWORD

by God

Despite Sarah's and my rather strained relationship over the course of her life, I am thrilled to be involved with this book. I've been tracking it from the day the deal was announced on Gawker to the moment I heard Sarah's first actual prayer to me. This happened roughly a week before the final deadline for the manuscript, and went something like,

> *Dear God, I know I have denied your existence my entire life, and have only spoken your name at crucial moments of jokes and orgasms, but I really need you now. I need you so much, in fact, that I want to accept you right now as my lord and savior, and renounce any negative things I've said about those who worship you. Please make this book be finished. I'll be honest: I kind of blew it off. I thought I could just knock the whole thing out in a week, but the assholes at HarperCollins never told me until JUST NOW that the font can't be larger than 12 point. I know I don't deserve your help, but I'm asking anyway. I can make it up to you. I'll even stop*

supporting abortion, if that's what you want. [LONG PAUSE.] Holy
crap, I am realizing . . . I am incredibly stoned. I ate half a brownie just
to ease my anxiety, but I think I went too far. This is always the problem
with pot cookies—you have no idea how potent they are 'til you eat one,
and by then it's too late late late. I'm making my own echoes echoes echoes.
I don't think I've ever been this high in my life. This is way too intense.
I'm really scared. I don't want to be alone right now.

At this point, she began to sob, and since I'm not completely heartless, I agreed to help her with the book. By no accident it came out
perfectly. But before we explore Sarah's life, a little about me . . .

No doubt you know the basics: I created the universe and everything in it from scratch—but oddly, I never tire of reminding
people.

What you might not know are my priorities. Given the sermons
and prayers of my followers, you might think I'm primarily interested in human suffering and punishing the wicked, but you'd be
mistaken. I mean, I follow what goes on in Darfur in the same way
I follow *Top Chef*. I'm totally interested, it's edge-of-your-seat stuff,
but if I forget to TiVo it, I probably won't bother buying it on
iTunes. For me, it's pretty much out-of-sight-out-of-mind-ish.

What holds my attention are things that I, personally, had a
direct hand in developing. Like, I'm really proud of cancer. Also
the HIV virus. I don't say that to provoke anyone, either. It's just
that at a basic scientific level, both of these inventions are really cool. They wield this enormous destructive power simply by
reproducing themselves, and no one can figure out how to stop
them. Locusts, flies, viruses, funguses—all that stuff just furi-
ously and egoless-ly copies itself until it dominates everything,
and it's all my work. So cool—so awesome to watch. Better, even,
than *Top Chef*.

Meanwhile, human beings are of diminishing interest to me. They seem to have developed priorities *other* than copying themselves. Namely, they all just seem to want to be on television. I can't make much sense of this, because I made sex more pleasurable for humans than almost any other species, except rabbits. That's not a cliché about rabbits—it's the truth. They fuck like meth-fueled monsters, and it's incredibly amusing to watch. But humans have taken on a strange habit of copulating in such a way that they don't reproduce. I was on YouPorn recently, and I was astonished by the places semen was landing—the hair, the eyes, the face, the toes, reading glasses, martini glasses. If this is what's in fashion, why *would* I care about Darfur? The entire human race is determined to let itself die out anyway—and in such a weird way. You'll never see cancer cells on the Internet smearing their genetic codes all over each others' cellular membranes. Cancer has a modicum of self-respect.

So that's more or less where my head is at these days.

Wait, just one more thing. I saw a video on YouPorn where two men managed to position themselves in such a manner that they could both penetrate the woman's vagina simultaneously! Regardless of what they think, let me just tell you where *I* stand on it: Let's not touch balls in a situation where we're working up to a cum. But that's just me. I'm not gay.

✻   ✻   ✻

As for Sarah Kate Silverman . . . she was born on December 1, 1970, the result of an eleven-and-a-half-minute-long period of revitalization in her parents' marriage, nine months prior. I took her life at the age of ninety-three as she was doing what she loved most—watching *Lost*. For her, it had not grown stale, even though fifty-three years had passed since the series finale.

After the blockbuster success of this book, Sarah was on a roll. She starred in a million hit movies, and even did a Tony Award–winning stint on Broadway. She released a CD of her own songs that went triple platinum and also collaborated with Ben Folds on an album which he maintained was *not* an "ironic choice."

Then on her forty-eighth birthday, a man in a suit appeared at Sarah's door, clutching a letter from the Alliance of Motion Picture and Television Producers. The letter thanked her for years of service to America but went on to note that, by industry standards, she could no longer technically be considered "cute" at this age, despite her thinness and youthful skin, and henceforth barred her from future work in show business. Like any Jewish girl made to feel insecure, she promptly developed an eating disorder that lasted until her next serious relationship.

In her late fifties, Sarah's career experienced a very brief bump. Due to changing demographics, network executives approached her with a show called *Wrinkles in Thyme* (her character's name was "Thyme"—"Thyme Stevens"). It was a sitcom about a washed-up actress being filmed for a reality show in which she returns to show business to star on a dramatic television series about a middle-aged woman looking to revive her acting career. The show ended when one of the editors committed suicide by impaling himself on another editor.

With her free time and large reserves of capital, Sarah devoted herself from there on in to rearing a brood of adopted children from—sigh, you guessed it—Africa. It might surprise you that I don't have more favorable things to say about Sarah's devotion to children. To be honest, I'm not that big a fan of kids. I had just one of my own, and I murdered him. So there's that.

Sarah had a much happier and more productive life than I'd ever intended for her. She loved dogs, New York, television, children, friendship, sex, laughing, heartbreaking songs, marijuana, farts, and cuddling. She hated everything else. Though she did not view it as one of her more interesting performances, I really loved her in *School of Rock*. And she was, for the record, the deciding factor in Barack Obama's victorious campaign for president of the United States. That alone makes her existence a net gain for the universe. I'm sitting five feet from Obama right now, and to be perfectly frank, I have a raging boner.

God,

December 1, 2063

THANKS-YOUS

THANK YOU FOREVER TO DAN STERLING WHO LENT HIS GENIUS TO ME AND WHOM I COULD NOT HAVE DONE THIS BOOK WITHOUT. YOU ARE A JEWISH BEACON, UNLIKE THE MANY JEWS WITH BEAKS-ON.

Thanks to HarperCollins president Michael Morrison, who allowed me to put Harris Wittels's penis in the book (see page 209); inspired designer Leah Carlson-Stanisic, who brought visual order to my verbal chaos; and, of course, my editor, David Hirshey, who for the last eighteen months has made me so fuckin' miserable by insisting that he knows what's funny (he doesn't), demanding that I meet my deadlines (I didn't), and valiantly defending the comedic merits of pee-pee versus pee (he failed). Though despite everything, he's kind of brilliant and he made this a much better book . . . Just don't eat with him because his chewing will make you want to stab yourself in your face.

*   *   *

Thanks to my family for their undying support and tolerance.

*   *   *

Thanks to Rick Kurtzman and Matt Snyder at CAA for telling me to write a book, and to Dan Strone of Trident Media for selling it.

*   *   *

Thank you, Robyn Von Swank, for your amazing cover photo— I'm a huge fan.

*   *   *

Thanks to Deanna Rooney for her graphic delights.

*   *   *

Thanks to my beautiful, spunky manager, Amy Zvi—you are my manager and my friend.

In that order.

xo

s